COLIN BAXTER ISLAND GUIDES

St Kilda

Dedication
To my sons, Christopher and Timothy, who also love wild
places and have endeavoured to keep me abreast of the times!

Acknowledgments
I must record my debt of gratitude to a number of people who have
willingly helped me in many different ways and in particular to Jon Warren for
introducing me to a number of documents which had escaped my attention. Thanks to
Andy Elwell for his contribution on the stacs. Peter Moore has shared his experiences
of the remoter parts of the archipelago. Andrew Currie has advised about the plant
list and Prof. Bill Lawson has guided me on a number of historical matters.
Christine Northeast has assisted with the text and my wife, Mary, has
shown unlimited patience and has given wise counsel at every stage.

Preparation for the Walks
The maps in this book give an indication of suitable routes to the interesting features on Hirta,
a larger scale map would be useful together with a compass. It is important to realise that some of the walks
are along cliffs of around 1,000ft which could be very dangerous in wet or misty weather, even dry slopes can be
slippery. It is helpful to discuss plans and conditions with the warden who can give up-to-date information and
permission where this is required. You are strongly advised to go in pairs and to tell someone of your route. In
damp weather, boots and waterproofs are essential. (A minister's wife who came to live on St Kilda with a
young family was horrified to find that the cliffs were not fenced!) Sensible precautions need to be
taken – the nearest rescue team is miles and hours away.

First published in Great Britain in 1995 by
Colin Baxter Photography Ltd
Grantown-on-Spey,
Morayshire, PH26 3NA
Scotland

Text © David Quine 1995
Drawings © David Quine 1995
Colour photographs © Colin Baxter 1995
Archival photographs on pages 14 and 19 reproduced courtesy of Bob Charnley collection
All rights reserved

Maps on p6/7, p22, p98, p110 and p122
Reproduced from the 1992 Ordnance Survey *St Kilda or Hirta* PATHFINDER 1373 map
with permission of The Controller of Her Majesty's Stationery Office © Crown Copyright.

British Library Cataloguing in Publication Data
Quine, David A.
St. Kilda. – (Colin Baxter Islands Guides)
I. Title II. Baxter, Colin III. Series
914.11404

ISBN 0-948661-58-5

Front Cover Photograph THE CLIFFS OF CONACHAIR WITH SOAY BEYOND
Back Cover Photograph VILLAGE BAY AND HIRTA FROM DÙN

Printed in Hong Kong

COLIN BAXTER ISLAND GUIDES

St Kilda

David Quine

Colin Baxter Photography, Grantown-on-Spey, Scotland

ST KILDA

The steadfast rock of the islands and stacs are all that remain of a
tertiary volcano which gave rise to the archipelago of St Kilda. Among the treasures
of these islands is its unique natural habitat, home to the native Soay Sheep and St Kilda Wren
– with breathtaking cliffs providing sites for a million nesting seabirds. Yet, here too are
traces of an isolated human existence, dating back some 4,000 years.

Contents

ST KILDA

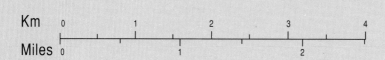

Km 0 — 1 — 2 — 3 — 4

Miles 0 — 1 — 2

N

HIRTA

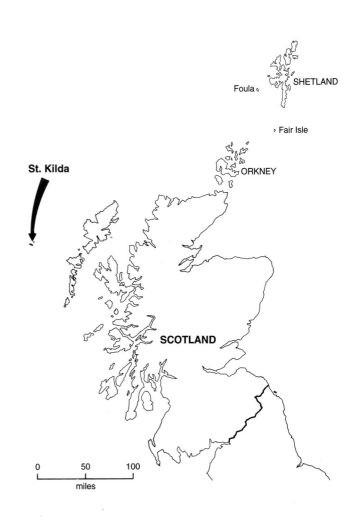

How to get there

THE VOYAGE

What a relief it would be to many if there were an easy way to reach St Kilda. A helicopter flight would be the quickest and most pleasant method, but this is not an option! A few have windsurfed and canoed the 50 miles from the Outer Hebrides, but most have to rely on a small boat. It is possible to charter a yacht or a converted fishing vessel or a schooner. Most boats leave from Oban which has the advantage of being a road and rail terminal. Others offer the shorter voyage, about 8 hours, from the Outer Isles.

The boat trip direct from Oban can take 22-48 hours or longer, depending on the route and the weather. The nearest way from Oban passes through the Sound of Mull, west of Rum and through the Sound of Canna, where some vessels stay the night.

From here the boat heads for the Neist Point of Skye and then north-west across the Minch at its narrowest stretch, perhaps to stay a night at Lochmaddy on North Uist, or Leverburgh on Harris. Then, passing through the Sound of Harris, the northern route heads due west for St Kilda. Some boats take the southern route and stay overnight at Lochboisdale, South Uist, before making for St Kilda.

It is unusual to reach St Kilda after a completely smooth crossing; practically unique to accomplish both outward and return journeys without hitting a rough spell. Village Bay is a safe haven provided an east wind does not arise; every skipper must be alert to the immediate and longer term weather conditions, and often a stay has to be terminated early to avoid a 16 hour journey against an easterly. John Reid, the skipper of the Jean de la Lune, speaks of doing the 'Ardnamurchan Waltz' and the 'St Kilda Two-step'.

Boreray and the Stacs look like a crouching lion from 'the Gap' on Hirta. Seen best in the glow of a late evening, or colourful dawn.

There are facilities for small numbers to camp on the main island. The National Trust for Scotland restricts the numbers so permission needs to be obtained before planning such a holiday. One of the best introductions to the archipelago is to join a St Kilda work-party when you are taken out by boat to stay on the island for two weeks. You assist with various conservation tasks as well as having free time to explore the main island. These parties, which are usually over-subscribed, are organised by the Secretary, St Kilda Club, National Trust for Scotland, 5 Charlotte Square, Edinburgh EH2 4DU.

A friend of mine recently told me of his experience on his first visit to St Kilda. Having left Lochmaddy in North Uist the boat passed through the quiet but tricky waters of the Sound of Harris, only to hit really rough seas and weather conditions in the Atlantic. He retired to his cabin and fell asleep. The boat ploughed her way through the 8 hour journey to reach Village Bay, St Kilda, only to find it was too stormy to land. The skipper reluctantly turned his craft and made the 50 mile voyage back, through the Sound of Harris. Soon after, as my friend emerged from his bunk and to his great relief saw land, he triumphantly exclaimed, 'St Kilda at last!' He was shattered by the reply, 'No, Lochmaddy!' He did in fact reach his destination a few days later! The first indications of 'islands ahead' as the boat leaves the Sound of Harris, with 50 miles of Atlantic waters still to negotiate, are small parties of gannets, returning from their fishing expeditions, overtaking the boat. They form an undulating line as they fly low over the sea, rising and falling with the crests and troughs, aiming straight for their island nesting sites. On a clear day wisps of cloud over Hirta and Boreray form a banner, streaming away east for several miles. At last, about one hour after leaving the isle of Shillay, two faint smudges can be picked out on the horizon: to the left is Hirta and to the right, Boreray. Beware, the curvature of the earth plays tricks with their shapes. To the south of Hirta appears a small stac (could it be Levenish?), followed by others, which surprisingly fuse to form the island of Dùn. Two stacs

Manx Shearwaters.
These birds nest in huge numbers in burrows among the rocks of Carn Mór and return under cover of darkness to avoid the attention of greater black-backed gulls. They have the weirdest call of all the British seabirds, the one in the burrow calling to its mate flying in. St Kildans would wait with their dogs to catch them.

seem to grow to the north of Boreray – one becomes An t-Sail, the other Stac an Armin.

To approach Boreray and sail under the magnificent 300m cliffs gives the finest introduction to the archipelago. Sheep are tiny dots on the steep grassy slopes and thousands of nesting and wheeling gannets reinforce the feeling of grandeur and a sense of scale. Further north are the extraordinary buttresses surmounted by contorted rock pinnacles, turrets and towers standing gaunt against the skyline. The fabulous view between Boreray and Stac an Armin follows where the whole of the island group is slowly and majestically revealed. Passing round and under the north end of Stac an Armin and gazing up the 200m vertical cliff is awe inspiring, yet the west cliffs of Boreray rise to twice this height. As the boat passes under the Casting Point of Stac Lee the scene becomes truly breathtaking and you are left quite speechless as you recall that the St Kildans crawled at night along these ledges to capture adult gannets.

Leaving Stac Lee, ahead lie Dùn, Hirta and Soay. The excitement increases as Village Bay is approached. In the bowl of the amphitheatre is the deserted Village with the cottages and blackhouses strung out along the street, the white Factor's House; the Kirk; the Manse; the Store, and the Army Camp. At last you see where the St Kildans worshipped, and eked out their existence on their crofts, and where they climbed the cliffs. We share the same feeling as Lachlan MacLean who arrived in the summer of 1838, 'I am at length, thank God, arrived on terra firma in St Kilda, the place of which, of all places within the British dominions, I longed most to see; and I had not certainly been led to form a false or exaggerated conception of it; nay, the half had not been told me.'

There is so much to explore.

View of the Archipelago – from the east.

After leaving the sound of Harris the archipelago is first seen as tiny specks on the far horizon, with an expanse of sea separating the two island groups, Hirta and Boreray. Later the individual islands become distinctive. Left to right – Island of Dùn, Mullach Bì, Oiseval, Conachair, Cambir, Island of Soay, Island of Boreray and Stac an Armin.

Island Background

GEOLOGY

On most maps St Kilda appears as a minute speck in the Atlantic Ocean. It came into being during the volcanic outbursts in the Tertiary Era, 54-65 million years ago, together with Rum, Ardnamurchan, Mull, north-east Ireland, the Faroes, Iceland and part of Greenland. At St Kilda there was a centre of plutonic activity between Hirta and Boreray, and great masses of molten magma were forced up from the earth's crust in several stages. The rim of the volcano is defined by Soay, the south and west coastline of Hirta, Dùn, Levenish and a submarine ridge continuing towards Boreray. A rock sample collected in 1967 was found to be 57 million years old and therefore a piece of the oldest known volcano of this period.

On approaching Village Bay one is immediately impressed by the rugged skyline of Dùn and Ruaival. These are formed from the oldest rocks, dark gabbro, which continue round to Mullach Bì and Soay, Boreray and the Stacs. In contrast, the more rounded shapes of Oiseval and Conachair are formed from the more recent rocks, the buff Conachair granite which weathers into massive slabs with ledges suitable for nesting fulmars. Between these masses is a complex central zone mainly of gabbros and dark dolerite sheets which can be seen cutting through many of the cliffs. The blue-black dolerite erodes more easily than many other rocks and is responsible for the formation of several caves around St Kilda.

Unlike the other Hebridean islands, Rockall and St Kilda were probably not covered by the main Scottish ice sheet during the last ice age. However, Hirta may have had its own small ice sheet to the east of Mullach Mór, reaching down to the shore of Village Bay and depositing a drift tongue. At the foot of Conachair is a clearly defined

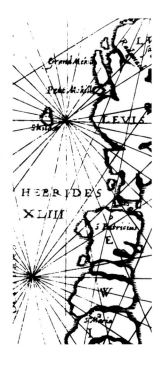

A map produced by Nicholas de Nicolay and published in his Chart of Scotland in Paris in 1583. St Kilda appears as 'Skildar'.

Looking over the small glen of An Lag, with its old sheep enclosures, across Village Bay to *Caolas an Dùin*, Dùn Passage. *Ruaival*, Red Fell, stands on the right.

pro-talus ridge formed from the rocks which have fallen from the steep face to land in or overshoot the hill foot bed of ice. An Lag is an example of an ice-deepened hollow which has been terminated by a moraine.

Subsequent rises in the sea-level have partly submerged the islands, and there are caves and a wave-cut platform up to 60m below the present surface. Millions of years after the original volcanic activity the shaping of the islands still continues today. Faults and weaker rocks are attacked by the elements, resulting in extensive rock falls and the formation of new sea-caves and sea-stacs. (Harding et al, 1984.)

A key to help in the identification of the rocks will be found in the appendix.

OCCUPATION

Sea-birds breeding in the summer and seals singing their songs in the caves must have occupied St Kilda well before Stone Age man, who arrived 4,000 years ago to make his

The Village Parliament. St Kilda's 'Parliament' was held opposite the Post Office. Here, the men of the island met to discuss their plans for the day.

The St. Kilda Parliament

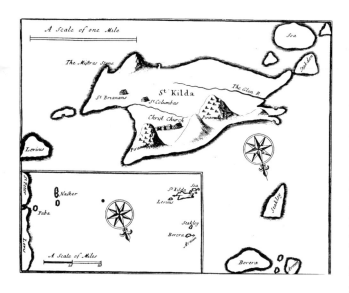

Martin Martin visited the islands in 1697 and produced the earliest known detailed map of St Kilda in 1698. He was tutor to the younger MacLeod of Dunvegan on Skye and was a great traveller and writer.

home on the main island. Since then successive occupants have left their marks in the form of a few stone monuments. Through the centuries man has visited or inhabited these islands, just managing to eke out an existence. The Vikings introduced the Field Mouse in their bundles of hay, probably inadvertently. They certainly made their mark in the place names of many of the hills and islands as well as leaving behind artefacts like a sword and two tortoise brooches. The island population reached a peak at the end of the 1600s when there were around 200 inhabitants. The smallpox outbreak in 1727 killed 94 people, and was a devastating blow to the community. However, the islands were repopulated from Skye, Harris and the Uists.

A steady decline in the population began with the emigration of 36 St Kildans to Australia in 1852 which reduced the total population to 74, with only 14 men over the age of 20 years. This was a crippling blow to the community. On Hirta, infantile tetanus, or eight-day sickness, was a menace, killing large numbers of babies during the next decades. Between 1856 and 1879, of the 62 babies born, 41 died of tetanus. Naval personnel from mainland Scotland served on the island during World War One and sowed ideas in the minds of the younger folk of an easier way of life in Glasgow. Four men died in one week in an influenza outbreak in 1926; the terrible winter of 1929-30 with near starvation followed by the deaths of two young girls on the island finally broke the St Kildans' spirit. They eventually capitulated at the evacuation on Friday 29 August, 1930. The island then lay uninhabited for 24 years.

OWNERSHIP

One of the earliest documents referring to the ownership of St Kilda dates from January 1373 when a charter was ratified by King Robert II enabling John, Lord of the Isles, a MacDonald, to present St Kilda and a number of Hebridean Islands to his son, Reginald. Later this group of islands was transferred to the MacDonalds of Sleat, on Skye. From this family it was to pass in the mid-fifteenth century to the MacLeods of Harris who had their seat at Dunvegan on Skye. It remained within the MacLeod clan until Sir Reginald MacLeod sold it in 1934 to the Fifth Marquis of Bute who bequeathed it to the National Trust for Scotland in 1956. It is now managed on their behalf by Scottish Natural Heritage and part is leased to the Ministry of Defence as a rocket tracking station.

From Bioda Mór, the summit of Dùn, looking north across Village Bay to Conachair and Oiseval, with Boreray (far right) four miles away in the distance.

The presence of the army detachment on the island makes life for the visitor both possible and pleasant, with the launch services and the Gemini crew, unlimited electricity, constant hot water, the use of freezers, a first-aid service, a weekly postal service, an opportunity to use the telephone, a shop and the 'Puff Inn'. The buildings, essential for maintaining the tracking station, have been painted grey to minimise the visual impact.

ISOLATION AND ADAPTATION

The isolated position of St Kilda, 50 miles out into the Atlantic and on the path of the storm belt which runs west to east, has made it difficult for plants and animals to obtain and maintain a footing on the archipelago. All the species which manage to do this successfully have made certain adaptations of structure or behaviour. This is reflected in the numbers of species on St Kilda compared with the mainland of Scotland and the inner Hebridean island of Rum:

	Mainland	*Rum*	*St Kilda*
Land vertebrates	38	9	2
Nesting birds	152	54	28
Plants	850	400	141

This isolation has also posed tremendous problems for man in establishing a settlement on St Kilda. The islands were literally cut off for eight or nine months of the year during the winter, the most difficult time to survive. The only communications link with the outside world was the unpredictable visit of the occasional trawler. It has been said that life on St Kilda in the winter was near that of hibernation.

Such isolation made the people independent, certainly in the earlier generations, and they developed an awareness of animal behaviour and did not over-exploit their environment. Over the years they also developed incredible skills, particularly on the cliffs, on which their very existence depended. Fortunately, Oliver Pike filmed them at work on the island in 1908 and 1910 and recounted the following: 'The natives were the finest climbers I have ever known; they were absolutely fearless on the steepest cliffs. I have seen them perform feats which would make our hair stand on end in fright. They worked in pairs, one man attached to a rope, and the other in charge at the top of the cliff. I watched one man take a run at a cliff, eight hundred feet high, with a sheer drop to the sea, fall face downwards when he reached the edge and, while his brother at the top allowed the rope to run through his hands, the climber actually ran down the cliff side, then, when the rope had almost run its full length, the one above put on the brake and the one below gave a twist, turned on his back so that he could see us above, and waved' (Pike, 1946).

FUTURE FEARS

In 1987 St Kilda was designated a World Heritage Site, the first in Scotland. The island group will receive special care and attention, but there are still threats. Everyone needs to be alert to the dangers of over-fishing, which caused such havoc amongst the breeding birds of Shetland in the late 1980s. The risk of oil spillage is another ever-present fear when a million visiting birds could be affected during the spring and summer. Another threat is posed by the brown rat which has decimated the wildlife on many other islands. These could be introduced accidentally by ships or tank landing craft. The Army are aware of this danger but continued vigilance is required by all.

THE VILLAGE 1860

This map is redrawn from the original made by Sharbau, a visitor to the Village in July 1858, and shows the occupants, field strips and cleitean with their contents.

On their Hebridean Tour in 1773, inspired by reading Martin Martin's book of 1698, *A Voyage to St Kilda*, Boswell reported a comment made by Dr Johnson: 'After dinner today, we talked of the extraordinary fact of Lady Grange's being sent to St Kilda, and confined there for several years, without any means of relief. Dr Johnson said, if M'Leod would let it be known that he had such a place for naughty ladies, he might make it a very profitable island.'

Though small and remote, the St Kilda archipelago is arguably the finest nature reserve in western Europe. Many who reach St Kilda, for whatever reason, will empathise with Lachlan MacLean after his visit in 1838.

> Wherever my lot may be cast,
>   my mind will ever revert to thee;
> unique in thy structure
> as in the manner of thy sons,
>   thou sittest queen of the Atlantic.

The Village.
Dated approximately 1884, this view of the village clearly shows the newer houses of stone with zinc roofs alongside the older, thatched blackhouses. The granite stone wall in front of the houses separated them from the cultivated strips.

Village, St. Kilda, from E.

Hirta, The Main Island

Nowadays the name St Kilda refers to the archipelago, and Hirta to the main island. However, the origins of these names are among the many mysteries which surround St Kilda. Three theories have been formulated. Martin Martin, who visited the islands in 1697, believed that the present name was derived from a man named 'Kildir' who lived on the island and after whom the well was named. Another suggestion, now under suspicion, is that it may have come from *kelda*, Old Icelandic for a well. 'Kilda' appeared on some of the first maps and the early settlement was centred on the *Tobar Childa*, which combines the Gaelic and Old Icelandic names for a well.

The most likely answer is that 'St Kilda' evolved through a copyist's error. *Skildir* is the Old Icelandic for 'shields' which could describe the shape of the islands when seen from a distance as they appear to rest on the surface of the water. 'Skildir' was marked on many of the contemporary Dutch and French maps, designed to assist fishermen to navigate in these waters, and 'Skildar' on that produced by Nicholas de Nicolay, published in Paris in 1583. On this map the 'R' was almost obscured by a bearing line on the page. It is thought that when Lucas J. Waghenear copied it he also separated the 'S' and the 'K', putting a full-stop in between them so that 'S.Kilda' appeared in his book of Charts published in 1592. An extraordinary story, but understandable as parts of the Uists were named S.Patricius, S.Culumbanus and S.Petrus on Nicholas de Nicolay's map. However, unlike the saints of the Uists, no 'Saint Kilda' has ever been recorded.

Hirta's derivation is less complicated and would appear to be from *hirtir*, Old Icelandic for deer. It is an imaginative description of the antler-like points of the stacs, peaks and pinnacles.

Looking from Claigeann Mór along the rugged western cliffs of Ruaival and Dùn.

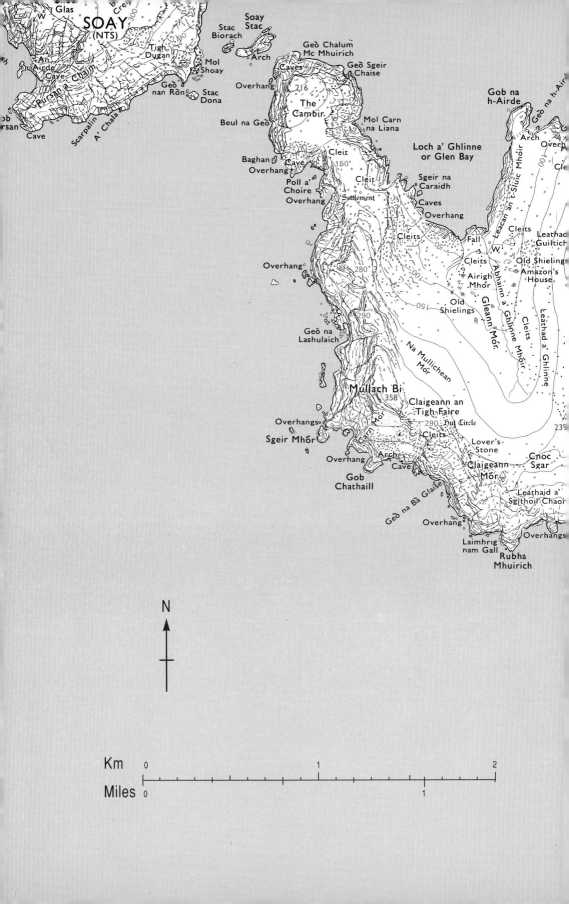

SOAY
(NTS)

Glas

An
Airde
Cave
Pursan a Chaim

Scarpalin

A' Chala

Cave

Geò
nan Ròn

Stac
Dona

Tigh
Dugan

Mol
Shoay

Stac
Biorach

Soay
Stac

Arch

Geò Chalum
Mc Mhuirich

Caves

Overhang

The
Cambir

216

Beul na Geò

Geò Sgeir
Chaise

Mol Carn
na Liana

Gob na
h-Airde

Geò na h-Airde

Arch

Overh

Cleit

Baghan
Overhang

Cave

Poll a'
Choire
Overhang

150

Cleit

Settlement

Sgeir na
Caraidh

Loch a' Ghlinne
or Glen Bay

Caves

Overhang

Leacan an t-Sluic Mhòr

Cleits

Leathac
Guiltich

Overhang

Cleits

Fall

W.

Cleits

Old Shielings

280

Cleits

Airigh
Mhòr

Amazon's
House

Abhainn a' Ghlinne Mhòra

Leathad a' Ghlinne

Old
Shielings

100

Gleann Mòr

Cleits

150

290

Geò na
Lashulaich

Na Mullichean
Mòr

Mullach Bì
358

Claigeann an
Tigh Faire
Hut Circle

290

239

Overhangs

Sgeir Mhòr

Carn Mòr

Cleits

Lover's
Stone

Cnoc
Sgar

Overhang

Arch

Cave

Claigeann
Mòr

Gob
Chathaill

Geò na Bà Glaise

Leathaid a'
Sgithoil Chaoi

Overhang

Overhangs

Laimhrig
nam Gall

Rubha
Mhuirich

N

Km   0   1   2

Miles   0   1

HIRTA

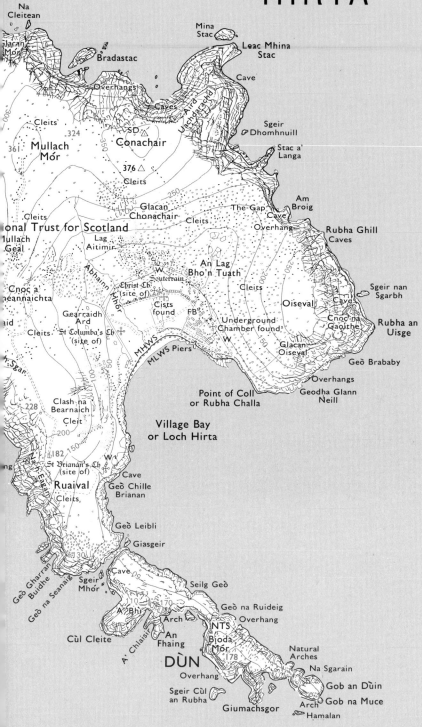

Na
Cleitean

Mina
Stac

Leac Mhina
Stac

Bradastac

Cave

Overhangs

Caves

Sgeir
Dhomhnuill

Cleits

SD

Mullach
Mór

.324

Conachair

361

376

Stac a'
Langa

Cleits

Am
Broig

Glacan
Chonachair

The Gap
Cave

Cleits

Overhang

Rubha Ghill
Caves

ional Trust for Scotland

Cleits

Mullach
Geal

Lag
Aitimir

Sgeir nan
Sgarbh

Cnoc a'
heannaichta

Abhainn Mhór

An Lag
Bho'n Tuath

Cleits

Oiseval

Cave

Christ Ch
(site of)

Souterrain

W

Rubha an
Uisge

Cists
found

FB

Cnoc na
Gaoithe

Gearraidh
Ard

St Columba's Ch
(site of)

Cleits

Underground
Chamber found

W

Glacan
Oiseval

Geò Brababy

h. Sgar

MHWS

MLWS Piers

50

Overhangs

228

Clash na
Bearnaich
Cleit

Point of Coll
or Rubha Challa

Geodha Glann
Neill

200

150

Village Bay
or Loch Hirta

182

St Brianan's Ch
(site of)

W

Ruaival

Cave

Cleits

Geò Chille
Brianan

Geò Leibli

Giasgeir

Cave

Seilg Geò

Geò Gharran
Buidhe

Sgeir
Mhór

Geò na Ruideig

Geò na Seanair

A' Bhì

Arch

Overhang

Cùl Cleite

A' Chlais

An
Fhaing

NTS
Bioda
Mór

Natural
Arches

DÙN

178

Na Sgarain

Overhang

Gob an Dùin

Sgeir Cùl
an Rubha

Arch

Gob na Muce

Giumachsgor

Hamalan

The Village

The earliest known monuments on St Kilda, the boat-shaped settings of An Lag, date back to around 1850 BC. Other ancient sites include the later earth-houses in the village and horned structures in Gleann Mór.

The medieval village was centred near the source of the Tobar Childa at the foot of Conachair. The present village was planned in 1834. The stimulus came from Sir Thomas Dyke Acland, sometime MP for Devon, who visited St Kilda in 1812 and 1834. He was horrified by the squalid conditions in which the St Kildans existed and left a gift of 20 guineas with the Minister, to be given to the first person who demolished his hovel and built a new house. The outcome was a newly planned settlement under the inspiration and supervision of the Rev. Neil MacKenzie, the Minister in residence from 1830 to 1844. The plan included a Head Dyke, a wall by the sea, a curving main street with 30 new blackhouses, each with a window, and some with extensions for other members of the family, an ash pit, a communal corn drying kiln, a saw-pit and a graveyard. Each house had a field strip running from the sea wall to the house and above the house to the Head Dyke. A low wall separated the strips. The villagers also built more cleitean, stone structures with turf roofs unique to St Kilda, which were designed for drying and storing hay, fuel and birds. The Kirk, Manse and Store were built shortly before this time.

The next stage in the development of the Village followed a gale in October 1860 which took the roofs off several of the blackhouses. The owners from Dunvegan Castle sent out their stone mason and work began on the first of the modern houses, of which 16 were eventually constructed between the blackhouses. The Factor's house was also built about this time.

One of the most impressive views on St Kilda is from 'the Chimney' at Clash na Bearnaich, which affords a bird's-eye view of the Village. An Lag in the distance leads up to the Gap and Boreray beyond.

25

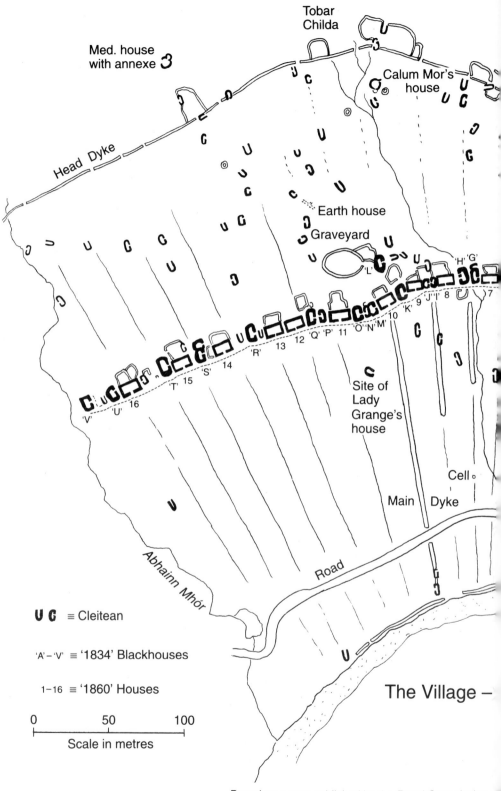

Tobar
Childa

Med. house
with annexe ♋

Calum Mor's
house

Head Dyke

Earth house

Graveyard

'L'

'H' 'G'

7

'J' 8
'K' 9
'N' 'M' 10
'O' 11
'P' 11
'Q'
12
'R'
13
14
'S'
'T' 15
'U'
16
'V'

Site of
Lady
Grange's
house

Cell

Main   Dyke

Abhainn Mhór

Road

U C ≡ Cleitean

'A' – 'V' ≡ '1834' Blackhouses

1–16 ≡ '1860' Houses

0   50   100

Scale in metres

The Village –

Based on a map published by the Royal Commission o

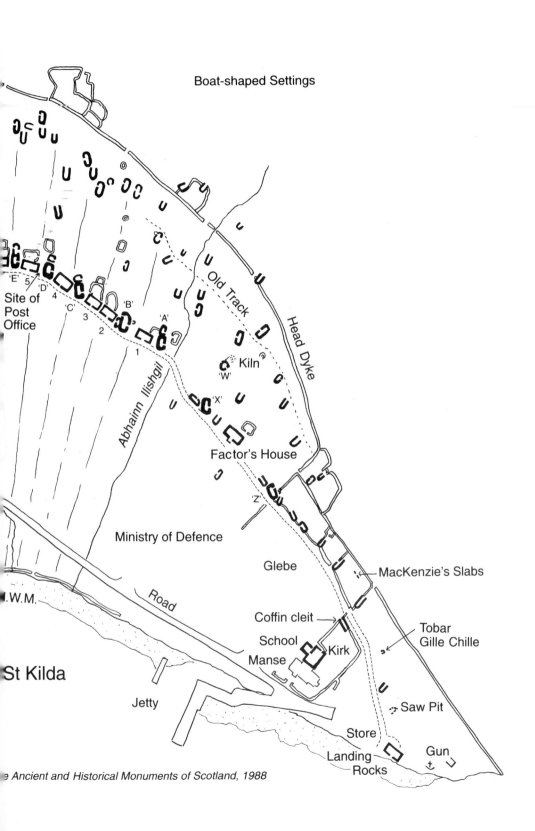

Boat-shaped Settings

Old Track

Head Dyke

Site of
Post
Office

'E' 5
'D' 4
'C' 3
'B'
2
'A'
1

Abhainn Ilishgil

'W'
Kiln

'X'

Factor's House

'Z'

Ministry of Defence

Glebe

MacKenzie's Slabs

L.W.M.

Road

Coffin cleit

Tobar
Gille Chille

School
Kirk

Manse

St Kilda

Jetty

Saw Pit

Store

Gun

Landing
Rocks

e Ancient and Historical Monuments of Scotland, 1988

Village Walk

Walk through the Village and look back 70 years; see the children going to school, the families busy on their crofts or attending the kirk, or maybe the 'Parliament' in session outside the post-office. Little has changed where the houses, kirk and store have been re-roofed. Other structures indicate the St Kildans' way of life, little bridges and rubbish pits, kiln and cleitean, walls, wells and old blackhouses, all beautifully constructed. The stones speak volumes, especially when the cloud is down on Conachair and the mist swirls round Oiseval. Allow one to two hours.

The walk begins at the Jetty.

THE JETTY

The jetty was not built until 1901. Before this everything had to be man-handled over the rocks and loaded into the six-oared Highland boats. The cargoes could include anything from barrels of fulmar oil, to catches from fishing

The Village Street is a haunting mixture of deserted stone dwellings: the rectangular shapes of the 1860s houses alongside rounded oblong 1834 blackhouses, the storage cleitean and a great maze of walls and enclosures.

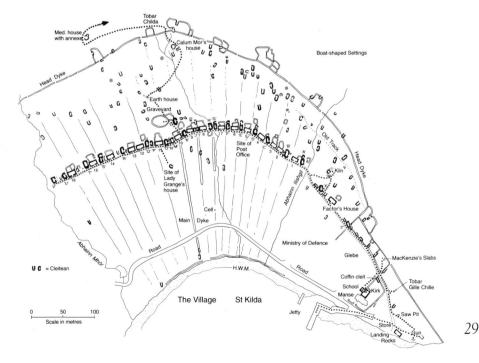

29

expeditions, to large boxes of eggs, to gannets from Boreray and the Stacs as well as live sheep from Soay and Boreray. From time to time even a bull began his journey this way. Boats were immediately hauled up over the rocks to safety above high tide, but this involved half the village population on each occasion. Sudden weather changes occasionally had catastrophic results. In 1759 when an October gale had raged for four days, the only boat was smashed to pieces as the men attempted to land. They had left a party on Boreray to survive the winter and be rescued in June of the next year.

The rocks near the present jetty were blasted in the 1860s to try to improve landing, but the work was not completed. Not surprisingly the islanders reported to the Napier Commission in 1883 that a pier would make all the difference to life on St Kilda. Eighteen years elapsed before the 'Congested Districts Board' produced a scheme and sent an engineer to spend the winter on St Kilda and to supervise the natives in the labour of excavation. The pier immediately made a tremendous difference as both stores and passengers could be landed off the *Dunara Castle* in spite of a south-easterly gale. In due course a winch enabled the boats to be brought up the slipway without involving many of the inhabitants, and a crane on the jetty eased the loading and unloading of goods.

Children played on the jetty during their morning break, winding their friends up in baskets using the crane! After the evacuation in 1930 the jetty was enlarged but it is still too shallow to allow even small trawlers or yachts to tie up; inflatables and dinghys are the only suitable users.

HEAD DYKE

One of the first tasks in 1834 was the construction of the Head Dyke, a huge wall using massive stones, to enclose the village and field strips and to keep out the sheep and cattle while crops were growing. Each house had a gap in the wall for access to the common grazing land outside the village enclosure. These gaps were closed up during the

Soay Ram. Soay Sheep are a very primitive breed resembling the Mouflon of Sardinia, probably brought to Britain by neolithic farmers and to St Kilda by the Vikings. They were found only on the island of Soay, but after the evacuation 107 were introduced to Hirta. Numbers now vary from over 1,700 to 600 in years when there is a food shortage.

spring and summer until the animals were permitted into the area after the crops had been harvested in the autumn. The wall extends for 1.5km and encloses 20 hectares (50 acres) of land.

Walk up the slipway from the jetty; the white building on the left was the manse. Keep to the right, heading east about 75m, the large slate-roofed building is the Store.

THE STORE

The Store (sometimes called the 'Feather Store') was erected by the owners, the Macleods of Skye, sometime before 1815, the year in which the geologist John MacCulloch visited the island and found that the Store was being used for church services. It may appear on Acland's painting of 1812. By 1822 Rev. Dr John MacDonald, the 'Apostle of the North', preached there. He called it 'the schoolhouse, which is also the only barn in the place, and a sort of common property'. It could hold all the 111 inhabitants, and on his visit in 1824 he taught a school of 57 which included 16-18 grown-up pupils. It was the first slated and two-storey building on St Kilda. Apart from worship and school it was used to store produce for export via the factor in lieu of taxes. In 1841 it was used almost entirely for bags of feathers of all kinds of birds – 240 stone, ready for export. At other times, it housed tweed, dried fish, barrels of fulmar oil, as well as the locals' fishing gear, and latterly, imported fuel, coal and paraffin, as well as oatmeal.

On 15 May 1918 the roof and front wall were severely

View from the boat in Village Bay. This gives a good introduction to the interesting structures on St Kilda. The distinctive street of 16 houses stretching along the bay, the hillside dotted with hundreds of cleitean and the profile of Conachair and Oiseval brooding over all. Left to right – Jetty, Manse and Church, Coffin Cleit, Tobar Gille Chille, Cleit, Saw-pit, Store, Gun; the Head Dyke lies at the back.

damaged by shells fired from a German submarine in an attempt to destroy the wireless aerial, which supplied information to the Navy. Seventy-two shells were fired, damaging the Kirk, the Manse, two cottages and two boats, but there was no loss of life. The roof and wall were not repaired until 1986 when new floors were also added to provide accommodation for those studying during extended periods on the islands.

GUN AND AMMUNITION STORE
Behind the Store, to the east, in response to the shelling by the German submarine, a four inch Mark III QF (Quick Firing) gun and ammunition store were installed between August and October 1918. The gun was made in 1896 – and was never used in anger!

Follow the track for about 25m, from the Store to the Village.

SAW-PIT OR SAW-DOCK
On the right of the track lying 5m uphill is the saw-pit. The Rev. Neil MacKenzie in the 1830s acquired a large two-man saw and set about building a saw-pit to make use of any driftwood washed up on the beach. He concluded after a number of years that it was rare to find good pieces: 'due to the rocky nature of the shore and the constant surf, they were generally ground to matchwood'.

The structure, in the shape of the hollow prow of a boat, uses local stone and was probably about 2m high to allow one man to stand on the ground and the other at the level of the log being sawn. It was used until about 1910 after which it was easier to import planks from Glasgow.

CLEIT
Close by the saw-pit is the first of the many cleitean which are such a prominent feature – dotted as they are all over the island – 1,260 on Hirta and a further 170 on the other islands. They are a St Kildan invention to wind-dry all sorts of things in a moist climate. They come in many shapes and sizes, but all have dry stone walls to allow the

One of the restored 1860s houses, as darkness begins to fall on the Village street.

wind to whistle through, and great stone slabs for roofs, capped with turf to absorb the water. In 1861 those in the village contained birds, fish, hay, manure – others had eggs buried in peat. Young live lambs were kept through winter in some of the cleitean and the manure cleaned out and put on the fields in the spring. In this century the cleitean within the Head Dyke were used to dry and store hay for winter feed for the cattle. This one, along with those in the Glebe, belonged to the Minister who had to cut hay for his cow, a time consuming occupation, with a little assistance.

TOBAR GILLE CHILLE, THE WELL OF THE SERVANT OF THE CHURCH

A few metres past the cleit and lying back from the track is *Tobar Gille Chille*, pronounced 'Tobar Ille Heelee'. There are many wells on St Kilda supplying cool, clear water as this one still does. It is protected by a well-constructed wall on three sides supporting a huge lintel.

33

Follow the track – on the left is the wall enclosing the Manse and Kirk.

BELL OF THE JANET COWAN

This is a replica of the ship's bell from the *Janet Cowan*. The original was stolen after the evacuation. The *Janet Cowan* was built in Greenock in 1861 and went on the rocks on St Kilda in April 1864 while on a voyage from Calcutta to Dundee with a cargo of jute. The crew landed in their small boats on the north-east side of the island and eventually made their way over to the village where they were looked after by the St Kildans for a week. The bell was used to call the inhabitants to worship.

Enter the Kirk by the door at the north end.

THE KIRK

St Kildans were devout Christians – in 1697 they had three churches. Christ Church, within the present burial ground, fell into disrepair before 1799 when worship was held in the parson's kitchen where he was 'seated on a bag of feathers with a barrel of fulmar oil by way of reading desk!'

The stimulus for the present Kirk on St Kilda came from the Rev. Dr John MacDonald, who visited St Kilda in 1822, 1824, 1827 and 1830.

Plans for the Kirk were drawn up by Robert Stevenson in 1820. Part of the money to erect it was

Coffin Cleit and Store.
The Coffin Cleit stands just above the Kirk. The St Kildans kept wood for their coffins in here, making them inside if wet. The store had been left untouched after the submarine shelling in 1918 until it was repaired and re-roofed between 1984 and 1987. Fishing gear, ropes, imported coal and grain were stored here as well as fish, feathers and fulmar oil for export.

St Kilda Field Mouse.
Unique to Hirta and Dùn, *Apodemus sylvaticus hirtensis* can be found in large numbers within the Village and anywhere else with dry stone walls. One colony inhabits the boulder beach in Village Bay, others the cliffs and Conachair. They are nearly twice the size of mainland mice, and were possibly brought in by the Vikings. They feed mainly on grasses and seeds, but also spiders, insects and any stores left unattended!

provided by the Society in Scotland for the Propagation of Christian Knowledge (SSPCK) but most of the £600 needed was collected by the Rev. John MacDonald. He came in person to install the Rev. Neil MacKenzie into the newly built Kirk and Manse on 4 July 1830. The design was simple and sturdy and had a rough causeway up the centre, rough pews without backs, a huge pulpit and a precentor's desk.

The Kirk was renovated by the carpenters who came to build the schoolroom in 1898. Their work included boarding in the walls of the kirk and laying a wooden floor. After the evacuation the Kirk fell into disrepair and it has taken a tremendous amount of time, energy and skill over a period of 20 years by Allan Aitken and Archie Maynard and their team of skilled workmen to bring it into its present beautiful state.

SCHOOLROOM

The Kirk gives access to the schoolroom which was added between 1898 and 1900. It has recently been restored and houses a small exhibition relating to the Kirk and School. The teacher's desk, pupils' seating, wall-maps and shelves give an authentic feel. From 1884 the Ladies Association of the Highland Society raised money to send teachers to St Kilda, and formal teaching began in a room in the Factor's House with English, geography, history, arithmetic and composition in the curriculum. Schoolmaster John Ross (1889) dreaded the onset of the winter where 'the medicine chest contained little but fulmar oil, castor oil, mustard and whisky!' From 1900 the school came under the Inverness County Council run as a 'side school' under the supervision of a teacher from Obbe School, on Harris.

Lessons were often interrupted by unusual situations – the children helping in the catching of the sheep, collecting bird's eggs, carrying and plucking fulmars during the harvest and illness due to influenza, mumps or the 'boat cold'. The people suffered from colds and other infections after the first boat arrived each season – they had little immunity to infections brought in by the crews and

passengers. A death on the island would close the school for a week.

Rejoin the main street. Inside the first enclosure on the right are:

MACKENZIE'S SLABS

From this enclosure, notice the massive stones built into the foundations of the Head Dyke, and two even larger stones, next to each other and up-ended. The Rev. Neil MacKenzie records how these two defeated even the strength of the St Kildans – they were simply too heavy to move when the ground was being cleared for agricultural purposes. To reduce their surface area on the plot they were put on end. MacKenzie recognised that they might confuse antiquaries in the future!

TOBAR A' MHINISTEIR, THE MINISTER'S WELL

Near MacKenzie's Slabs, to the west of the track, is the

The Village from Conachair. Low light picks out the multitude of individual structures either side of the village street and Head Dyke.

Minister's Well, not visible now, as it has been incorporated into the buildings of the Ministry of Defence as the main supply of water for the camp and visitors.

NATIONAL TRUST FOR SCOTLAND CAMPSITE
Permission to camp must be obtained from the NTS and is limited to the last enclosure in the Glebe, east of the track. Within the enclosure, situated in the north-west corner, is an unusual cleit. It has a small doorway with seven steps down into the chamber below ground level but beautifully dry – a useful cooking cleit for campers! The next building is blackhouse 'Z' (a 'cottar house', being without land) which belonged to Roderick Gillies when it was first built.

Carry on up the track to the Factor's House.

FACTOR'S HOUSE
The Factor's House was probably built in the late 1860s on common land. It has a protecting porch and a second storey round the back providing sleeping quarters. It was built for the use of the factor from Dunvegan during his short stays to collect the rent from the St Kildans. It was used for some time as the school. Many interesting people have stayed in the upper room including John Sands, a journalist who was marooned for six months on his second visit to St Kilda in 1876 and wrote of and illustrated his experiences in *Out of This World*. Other notable early visitors include the Kearton brothers, photographers and naturalists, and Norman Heathcote, author and painter, as well as the resident nurse. Now it is home to the Warden who has his own photographic display on the wall. On occasion, he also uses the bath to keep young puffins in after weighing and ringing, before releasing them at dawn.

Just opposite the Factor's House is a post hole for one of the aerials for the radio which was used during the World War One and which was destroyed by a German submarine.

Continue a few metres up the track, past the cleit beyond the

Factor's House. The next building is:

RACHEL MACCRIMMON'S BLACKHOUSE 'X'

For 81 years Rachel MacCrimmon lived in a blackhouse.
She was one of the island's great characters, the only one
who refused to move from her 1834 blackhouse
into one of the 'modern houses' built in the
1860s. A photograph taken in 1910 shows her
outside the door with her spinning wheel. It is
a typical blackhouse – note the thickness of
the walls. Opposite the door was a stall for
her cow and nearby one for the sheep, a
grated hole allowed waste products to drain away
to the agricultural plot; her hens also had free access to the
house. The living quarters to the right consisted of one big
room with a central open fire. To conserve space, like
many, she had a bed in the wall, a 'crub' with a mattress of
the chaff of oats – the old-fashioned way. People would
retire into these like a puffin returning to its burrow.

    Despite the disadvantages of poor light, smoky fire
and the close proximity of the animals, these blackhouses
were designed for the terrain and were cosy, well insulated,
and end on to the prevailing wind, with rounded corners to
cut down the whistle of the wind.

Make a diversion, beyond Rachel's house, up the hill, past a
cleit, 20m in all to:

CORN DRYING KILN AND BLACKHOUSE 'W'

The corn drying kiln was discovered and excavated in
1989. On the left is the threshing floor with winnowing
window to the north-west, and, to the right, a flue curves
its way from the doorway and under a large lintel into the
bowl for the fire. A grill would rest on top of the bowl and
the corn would be dried in the sheaf before being threshed.
A common kiln was in use when Martin visited the island
in 1697 and another visitor commented on it in 1841.
However, archaeologists believe that this one was not used
over a long period, possibly owing to seepage of water. It

Graveyard Stones.
To mark a burial site,
rough natural stones
collected from the foot of
Conachair were erected.
These are now covered in
patterns by lichens. There
are only about five hewn
headstones with names.

certainly wasn't in use in the 1860s. In 1779 they had a small kiln underground to manufacture salt, used to preserve the birds. Abutting the threshing floor to the south-west is blackhouse 'W', the home of Effie MacCrimmon, the last of the great *senachie* or verbal historians, who died in 1869.

Return to the main track and continue north-west.

DRY BURN OR *ABHAINN ILISHGIL*, DEEP STREAM OF THE SPRING

The Dry Burn rarely lives up to its anglicised name, however, the stream will quickly reflect any rainfall. It carries water down from *An Lag Bho'n Tuath*, the hollow in the north, away into Village Bay. A considerable amount of energy has been expended in lining the bottom and sides with stone in the past. A little bridge leads to the Village proper and the main street.

HOUSE No. 1 – MACKINNONS

The old 1834 blackhouse 'A' and extension is situated to the east of the 1860 house. The latter has been re-roofed and made habitable, providing a dining-kitchen and leader's room for NTS work parties. The St Kildans often

Rachel MacCrimmon's Blackhouse. Rachel refused to accept a modern 1860s house, convinced that hers was far better adapted to the weather conditions on St Kilda. The house was shared by her cow and hens.

complained about the new houses – the insulation in the roof was poor and lost heat, the windows faced the sea and the storms, the walls had sharp corners and were higher, making them cold, windy and noisy. The original roofs of 1860 were made of zinc, but 'when it rained outside, it also rained inside!' Zinc was later replaced by felt and tar; even today this has to be renewed every 3-5 years.

At the time of the evacuation in 1930 this was the home of Norman MacKinnon and his wife Annie (daughter of Finlay Gillies of No. 7). Together with their eight children: Norman, Donald Ewen, Finlay, Rachel, John, Christine, Mary and Neil they were the largest family on St Kilda. Mr MacKinnon was considered to be the most skilful tailor on the island, and he was also the precentor at the services in the Kirk after 1924. The family was very short of food in the hard and prolonged winter of 1929-30 and were eager to leave before another winter.

HOUSE No. 2 – MACQUEENS

Finlay MacQueen lived alone here, his wife Mary, nee MacKinnon, had died before the evacuation. His daughter Mary Annie was married to Neil Ferguson junior, while his daughter Annie married Donald Gillies who lived at No. 13. Finlay had lived with his son Donald for some time before he left the islands, as did his son Norman and daughters Bessie and Christine. Finlay was a distinguished looking man, tall with a long black beard. He was proud of the puffins and gannets which he had stuffed and was one of Britain's greatest cragsmen and fowlers, accompanying Heathcote on his visit to the islands and stacs in 1898. Understandably he was one of the few who were reluctant to leave Hirta in 1930. This house is now a dormitory for the NTS work parties.

HOUSE No. 3 – MACDONALDS

This house was empty at the time of the evacuation. It had been the house of a remarkable family of MacDonalds who had lived on St Kilda since 1753. William MacDonald, who suffered greatly from asthma, was the first person to

Looking across the Village and its many cleitean, towards the screes of Conachair.

evacuate his whole family, which he did in 1924. He was a taxidermist and sold specimens to Manchester Museum, he was also the precentor until he left the island. William had married Mary Ann MacQueen in 1895 and had eleven children, John, Finlay, Annabella, Mary, Mary Betsey, Finlay John, Callum, Kirsty, Rachel, Marion and Mae. His brother, 'John R', left with him but was to return to live at No. 9. William's father, Neil, had married Isabella Ross Munro, the servant of the Rev. John MacKay, and his grandfather Callum had married Betsey Scott from Lochinver in 1834, the servant of the Rev. Neil MacKenzie.

Corn Drying Kiln.
This kiln was discovered and excavated in 1989. It probably went out of action due to seepage of water. It is beautifully preserved with its bowl, lintel and flue. Next to it is a threshing floor.

The house is now an extremely well laid out Museum with artefacts, photographs and documentary evidence about life on St Kilda as well as information on the flora and fauna. Many hours can be spent here on a wet day, or a dry one – and the heating is a great boon!

HOUSE No. 4 – FERGUSONS

This house was empty at the evacuation – it had been the home of Donald Ferguson and his wife Rachel (nee Gillies). Of their four children, Alexander had become a successful cloth merchant in Glasgow; Neil was the Postmaster on St Kilda; Annie married John Gillies senior of No. 15; and Donald became a minister in the Free Church, keeping up his love of boats and often returning to St Kilda. It is now a dormitory for NTS work parties.

HOUSE No. 5 – FERGUSONS

This was the home of the Postmaster Neil Ferguson, senior, and his wife Annie, the half sister of Finlay MacQueen; also living with them were his son, Neil and his wife Mary Anne (MacQueen), the last couple to be married on St Kilda. Neil, senior, was not only the Postmaster, but also the school manager, the flockmaster, store-owner and ground-officer of the estate. At the evacuation he took up a job with the Forestry Commission on the Tulliallan Estate. The house is now used as a store for the work parties.

POST OFFICE

Immediately to the east of House No. 5 was the Post Office. The flat grassy area was the base for the structure. The steps up to the door still remain. A sub-post office had been established in the Factor's House in 1890 and was administered by the Free Church Minister, the Rev. Angus Fiddes, at a salary of £5 a year, with some bonuses. When he left in 1905, Neil Ferguson took on the appointment which he held until the evacuation. The site was moved from the Factor's House in the summer of 1913 to a corrugated iron hut adjoining the east end of Neil's home. This was done to provide space for the Marconi Wireless Telegraph Company radio transmitter – gifted by the *Daily Mail* to the inhabitants. Neil and the missionary were responsible for operating the transmitter in the early stages. but in May 1918 it was hit by the shells from a German submarine, so St Kilda was once again cut off from the world. The St Kilda Parliament was held opposite the Post Office, where the men discussed the plans for the day. MacGregor (1969) commented, 'neighbouring Boreray was the limit of their foreign policy'.

1834 Improved Blackhouse. These were built in the few years following 1834 with walls nearly 2m thick. They were the first houses on the island to have windows; the cow resided at one end in the winter and helped the central heating; the 'crub', or bed was built into the wall to save space. Some had a 'granny flat', as in this sketch.

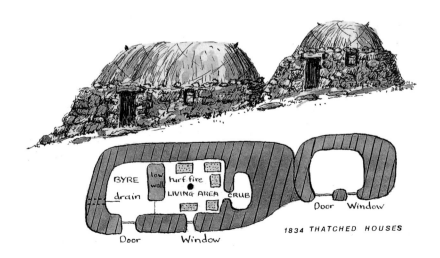

1834 THATCHED HOUSES

43

HOUSE No. 6 – GILLIES

The house was empty at the evacuation, Angus Gillies and his wife Annie had both died well before 1930.

HOUSE No. 7 – GILLIES

At the evacuation Finlay Gillies lived here (his wife Catherine and his son, Neil, had both died previously) with Neil's widow Katie and her two boys, Ewen and Donald. Finlay had accompanied the Kearton brothers on their visit in 1896. He was a good man, liked by all, and the oldest of the inhabitants, being in his 74th year at the time of the evacuation.

CONSUMPTION DYKE

On the low side of the street is the first of the 'consumption dykes', named as they were built to consume the stones when the agricultural plots below the houses were cleared. There are three, the third of which reaches down to the sea wall. Some have cleitean built into them.

Mist and rain add a little something to the atmosphere of the Village Street and its ruined buildings.

HOUSE No. 8 – MACDONALDS

The house was empty at the evacuation, as Callum MacDonald, known as 'Old Blind Callum', had died earlier. He had been married twice, first to a cousin, a MacDonald of No. 16, and later to Annie Gillies, a daughter of Norman Gillies and sister of Finlay. His son Donald and daughter Annie both left before the evacuation. He had been a quiet, retiring person who took great pleasure in the Sunday services; in the absence of the missionary and the elder he would preach at these.

The house was built for John MacDonald. Recent archaeological work at the east end of the house has revealed that it was constructed over his earlier blackhouse which was partly destroyed in a hurricane in 1860. The blackhouse had drains underneath, and some of the hearth stones and the wall footings remain in place and can be seen today.

A tar-boiling site has been discovered in the garden. Pre-blackhouse deposits include a midden, densely packed with bones, principally of seabirds but some of cattle and sheep. Leather shoes, 550 pieces of coarse pottery, one dated around 1685AD by thermoluminescence (TL), glass and 150 stone tools (pounders etc), and a small spindle whorl of steatite (possibly Viking) have also been found.

OLD MILL MARKED ON 1861 MAP

Between houses no. 8 and no. 9 are two blackhouses 'I' and 'J', the first with a small window towards the sea which is unique. In the passageway between them at the far end is a large window without a lintel, this could be a winnowing window to allow the wind free access for the disposal of the chaff; below is a large flat slab at a higher ground level, possibly the last vestige of a winnowing floor. The next blackhouse has its door opposite the first and also has a window with a lintel formed by two stones facing up towards Conachair – again, unique. It is marked on the map as a 'mill erected 1861'.

HOUSE No. 9 – MACDONALDS

J. R. MacDonald, the brother of William from No. 3, left
with the rest of the family in 1924. He obtained
a job on one of the drifters but later returned
to live here. Also living here were Annie
Gillies (Mrs Scalpay Gillies), whose
husband Ewen had died previously in a fall
from the rocks beyond Mullach Mór, and her
daughter Mary Anne.

Earth House.

This souterrain is the only
one preserved on St Kilda.
A house or store entirely
underground, it was
discovered by Sands in 1876
complete with floor, drain
and two annexes.

    The next blackhouse 'K' is where Betty
Scott, who came from Lochinver to be the
servant of the Rev. Neil MacKenzie, lived after
she married Callum MacDonald in 1834. She lost her
life on the *Dargavel* on the way to Harris.

*Pass blackhouse 'K' and turn right up a broad grassy path which
leads up to the graveyard.*

GRAVEYARD AND SITE OF CHRIST CHURCH

The massive stone wall in an oval form contains the
graveyard. It was built in the 1830s under the careful
supervision of the Rev. Neil MacKenzie who adds
poignantly, 'It was the portion of our work in which I took
the greatest personal interest, as there I buried three of my
children who died in infancy.' Most of the graves are
simply marked by rough stones selected from the foot of
Conachair, now well covered by numerous colourful
lichens.

    When Martin visited St Kilda in 1697 there were
three chapels in existence – St Brendan's on the way over
to Ruaival, St Columba's beyond the end of the main street
and across the recent tarmac road (see *Walk to Ruaival*) and
Christ Church which was situated within the present
graveyard. It was a stone building and measured 8 x 4m
with a roof similar to the old houses. It had fallen into
disrepair before 1799 and was rebuilt on its present site just
before 1830.

Return down the grassy path to the main street, noticing the well-made pit and garden belonging to House no.10.

HOUSE No. 10 – MACQUEENS
Donald MacQueen lived here but left to go to Glasgow before the evacuation. At the back of the house is a well-walled garden and excellent rubbish pit.

Pass the two blackhouses, 'M' and 'N' (back to back), and look in the next one, 'O'.

BLACKHOUSE 'O' – MACQUEENS
This was the home of Finlay and Chirsty MacQueen before they emigrated with their family on the *Priscilla* in 1852. Half of the 36 St Kildans died on the way or during the period in quarantine. Their son Malcolm recorded his memoirs (see *St Kilda Portraits*).

MacQueen's Blackhouse 'O'. The large cleit is the site of Lady Grange's house where she lived while she was exiled for eight years. Dùn, in the distance, forms the rugged breakwater protecting Village Bay.

Their great-great-grandson Kelman MacQueen and Kelman's cousin Scott MacQueen returned in 1990 from Australia to trace their roots. Kelman stood inside the doorway which faces east, and was amazed that the lintel was still over the doorway and another over the window although no-one had lived here since 1852.

HOUSE NO. 11 – MACQUEENS

Mrs Christine MacQueen lived here alone at the time of the evacuation. Her husband Norman had been drowned with Lachlan MacDonald's father in a boating accident off Dùn in 1909. She was aunt to Norman MacKinnon, senior, and had no children.

SITE OF LADY GRANGES'S HOUSE

About 25m below house No. 11 is the possible site of the house of the unfortunate Lady Grange, where she spent eight years (1734-42) of her forced exile. The house itself was destroyed some years before 1876 but tradition has it that it was on this site where the large cleit (No. 85) now stands. The door was added in the 1970s.

Lady Grange had been happily married for 25 years to James Erskine of Grange, brother of the earl of Mar, one of the Lords of Session. Her husband was a Jacobite and feared that she had heard too much intrigue, so he had her 'spirited away to the isle of St Kilda, [and] gave out that she was dead and celebrated her funeral'.

Lady Grange was eventually transferred to Skye in 1742 when a rescue bid was foiled and she died in a miserable hut at Trumpan in 1745.

HOUSE NO. 12 – GILLIES

This house was empty at the evacuation. Ewan Gillies, son of Norman, lived here until August 17th 1916 when he fell from the rocks in a tragic accident with John MacDonald, after which Ewan's widow Annie and daughter Mary Anne moved into No. 9.

HOUSE NO. 13 – GILLIES

At the evacuation Donald Gillies, son of John Gillies senior, lived here with his wife Christine and two daughters, Kathie and Rachel.

HOUSE NO. 14 – GILLIES

Mrs Annie Gillies was living here at the evacuation with her two daughters Rachel and Flora; her husband Donald

Cleitean are the St Kildan's unique structures used for drying and storing hay, birds, fish, and manure. They come in all shapes and sizes.

had died of appendicitis while minding the sheep on Boreray on June 16th 1922. Two other daughters were to die on St Kilda, Chrissie of mumps aged 13 in 1926 and Mary of TB on July 21st 1930.

This sad event confirmed to the islanders that they were doing the right thing in asking to leave the island.

HOUSE NO. 15 – GILLIES

At the evacuation John Gillies junior was living here with his son, Norman John (his wife Mary, nee MacQueen, had died of appendicitis in February 1930). Also living here was John's mother Annie (Granny Gillies, sister of Neil Ferguson senior), known as the Queen of St Kilda. Her husband, John Gillies senior, called Red Gillies on account of the unusual colour of his beard, was a powerful preacher and had a very strong voice. This had saved his life when he called for help in a boating accident off Dùn. He died in 1926 during an outbreak of influenza.

They had produced a remarkable family of five sons –

Donald who lived in No. 13 died aged 83; John; Neil, who left St Kilda in 1919 and worked in Glasgow as a ship's wheelwright, was employed on St Kilda as bird watcher by Lord Dumfries from 1931-9 and died aged 93 in 1989; Donald John was ordained and spent most of his life in Canada and died aged 92; Donald Hugh (Ewen) died on the island in 1925 aged 25.

Beyond the next blackhouse 'T', on the upper side of the Main Street, is a lovely well from which the Gillies family collected their buckets of water. Stone slabs form a bridge across the street.

HOUSE NO. 16 – MACDONALDS

Rachel MacDonald – nee MacKinnon – lived here at the time of the evacuation – her husband Donald died in a terrible boating accident off Dùn in March 1909, together with the two MacQueen brothers, Norman and John. Rachel lived with her sons Ewan and Lachlan. She was extremely kind and generous. Ewan was chosen by Cockburn, a geologist, to be his companion in his surveying work in 1927-8, at the evacuation he was leaving the island for the very first time. Of the other children, Rachel had died on St Kilda, Donald and Angus left around 1920, Donald became a lay preacher, Angus died in 1980. Lachlan was 24 years old at the evacuation and had vivid memories of life on the island and a wonderful sense of recall and humour. He loved to talk about the islands

Bull House. This building housed the village bull during the winter. Each family took it in turn to feed the valuable animal.

and returned to them until 1987. He died in December 1991 aged 85.

Built into the front wall of the house is an Early Christian carved stone cross, possibly seventh century, lying in a horizontal position to the right of the east window. Another carved cross was discovered in the slabbed roof of Cleit 74. Inside the house are alcoves in which Donald MacDonald had made his own wooden cupboards.

The blackhouse 'U' to the west was used as a byre, a wooden partition separated the cattle area and a bedding area for a young bullock, and a drain led through to the agricultural plot. The other side of the partition was used for threshing the corn (oats) and barley and for storing fodder for the cattle, seed potatoes, barley, and coal from the trawlers. To the west of the blackhouse is a tall well-made cleit which was used for drying hay from the croft. Further west is another very old blackhouse, 'V,' with no window but a well-made wall cupboard. In Lachlan MacDonald's day the roof was thatched just like the byre and lambs were kept there during the winter – they were let out during the day but soon learnt where to return at night.

Medieval House with Beehive Annexe. This is one of the most striking buildings on St Kilda. It was originally a house with a low tunnel through to a beehive chamber. It had an open window, with both parts covered by turf. It was used by St Kildans in this century for the storage of hay.

THE OLD VILLAGE

Retrace your steps along the main street and turn left between houses 9 and 10 up the track towards the graveyard. Turning right work your way to the north side of the graveyard wall. Continue a few metres until, facing Conachair, you stand in line with the remnants of an old wall. Turn left and walk for 45 metres to the Earth House.

Looking down from Conachair on the Village below, with Oiseval to the left and the long ragged arm of Dùn to the right.

EARTH HOUSE, *TAIGH AN T-SITHICHE,* HOUSE OF THE FAIRIES

Taigh an t'sithiche – pronounced, 'Toy na she-ish'. The Earth House or souterrain is possibly the earliest building in the village, thought to date back to between 500 BC and AD 300. It is in the form of a straight underground passage with two annexes off to the right. The walls are made of very large stones which converge towards ground level to support the slab-like lintels which form the roof. In 1876 Sands, the earliest excavator, found 'a large quantity of limpet shells bearing the marks of fire, bones of sheep and cattle, seafowl chiefly those of the Fulmar and the Solan Goose'. The St Kildans called it *Taigh an t-Sithiche*, the House of Fairies. It was thought to have been a house or hide-out, but recent theories suggest it was an ice house for the storage of food. Another earth-house was discovered by MacKenzie in 1830 in the small central area behind the glebe, but he covered it up again.

Return to the same place by the graveyard wall, look half right to the gap in the Head Dyke (not the one immediately ahead), a few metres to the right is a cleit built into the Head Dyke, just below this is a grassy mound – Calum Mór's house.

CALUM MÓR'S HOUSE
Calum Mór's House may date back to around AD 600. It is oval in shape, and measures 4 x 3m and over 2m in height. The immense size of the stones has led to the story that it was built by a local strong man, Big Calum, who had not been permitted to go to Boreray with the fowlers. To demonstrate his frustration and strength he used massive stones to erect his house in one day!

TOBAR CHILDA
Through the gap in the wall above Calum Mór's House is the source of the Tobar Childa within a few metres of the Head Dyke. Two main springs give a steady supply of lovely clear water, and in wet weather there may be as many as five in the area. The two main springs give rise to the two streams which merge about 20m below the Head Dyke and then zig-zag down to the village through a lush growth of irises. The lower part of the stream is lined and walled with stones. The Tobar Childa supplied water for the old village which was centred on dry ground near and above the springs.

SHEEP SHEARING AND DIPPING
The sheep were run down, one at a time, in an exciting manner, with the help of children and dogs: they called it *Ruagadh* – 'the chase'. Shearing consisted of simply

53

plucking off the wool with a pen-knife leaving the sheep looking in a sorry state. George Murray, the schoolmaster from 1886-7 and who kept a detailed diary of his stay, attempted to introduce new shears. St Kildans called them 'the new invention' and their response to the quick but noisy machine was – *O graidh! na gearr an sgornan*, 'O Love, don't cut the throat'. *Na toir as a' grudhan*, 'Don't take the liver out'.

The Tobar Childa supplied water for the sheep dipping which was carried out a few metres to the west. The St Kildans made a temporary triangular sheep fank, using the Head Dyke on the lower side and trawl netting linked to a cleit on the other two sides. A tarred wooden box with a ramp was filled with water and chemicals for the dip. The sheep were collected up from below the Lover's Stone, Ruaival, Conachair and Oiseval. Those from the Cambir and Gleann Mór were taken to a fank at Gob na h'Àirde. Each year a policeman came from the mainland to supervise the operation.

THE OLD VILLAGE

In the area above the Tobar Childa and to the west there is a tremendous amount to see of the vestiges of the old village. There are remains of old field walls, enclosures, little sections of old tracks and cleitean of all shapes and sizes – small hemispherical (thought to be the oldest), double deckers, and some with beehive annexes, which implies the site of a house which has now been modified and extended into a cleit. Explore the whole area in depth if time allows. The only beehive annexe still intact is in what was called the Medieval House, now Cleit No. 122-3.

MEDIEVAL HOUSE WITH BEEHIVE ANNEXE

The 'Medieval House with Beehive Annexe' is situated 70m west of the Tobar Childa. It is now referred to as Cleit 122-3 but deserves a more attractive title! The 'House' is now considered to have been modified and enlarged to form a cleit with a high doorway and splendid corbelling. On the outside it is buttressed on the south side and turfed on the top. There is a little low connecting tunnel through which it is possible to wriggle to the cell or beehive annexe which was possibly used for sleeping quarters. It has a lintelled window.

Above the Medieval House with the beehive annexe there is a cleit, from this follow the old wall north-east, continue up to the top edge of the main cluster of buildings and pick up the old track.

Calum Mór's House.
This imposing structure, made from massive stones, has a low doorway, but plenty of headroom inside. The whole house is covered with turf and there are traces of two attached beehive annexes.

OLD TRACK TOWARDS THE JETTY

In fact there are two old tracks running more or less parallel working their way in the direction of the jetty. Both of these give commanding views of the whole of Village Bay, with the villages – old and new. It is worth making a diversion to the Bull's House.

BULL'S HOUSE

The Bull's House is a roofless, rectangular building with very thick walls and a door to the east, quite different from any cleit. It is situated in the old village area, outside the Head Dyke, in direct line with the wall remnant emanating from the graveyard.

The community bull grazed with the cattle during the summer months but in the winter time was kept in the Bull's House which had a wooden roof covered with straw, not turf. The crofters took it in turns to feed him, a fortnight at a time. There were no scales on St Kilda for weighing; instead, one long piece of rope was used in turn by each family to tie round the bundles of hay, to ensure that the feeding was shared equally.

Follow the old track and gradually work down through the Head Dyke to the Jetty.

55

Oiseval Walk

Oiseval is Old Icelandic for east fell, pronounced by the St Kildans as 'Oysheval'. It is a huge domed mass of buff coloured Conachair granite covered by varying amounts of vegetation. To the seaward side it looks as if a giant has clawed his finger nails down the rocks and then sliced the cliffs by the Gap with a vertically held knife! This walk encircles Oiseval and visits the Gap. Allow two to three hours.

Begin near the Jetty and walk east past the Store and the gun emplacement, follow the rising low cliff edge above the end of the beach and cross the end of the Head Dyke. Care is needed as cliff falls have left overhangs.

PEREGRINE FALCON

The great hump of Oiseval, East Fell, from Dùn.

Stand by the Head Dyke and scan the sky. Occasionally a peregrine falcon can be seen performing impressive aerial manoeuvres over Oiseval, then stooping sharply and skimming over the wall, frightening a group of

oystercatchers feeding among the cleitean by the Factor's House. These scatter in all directions, 'kleeping' excitedly as they disperse. On my last visit the peregrine rose again, soared to gain height and this time irritated a couple of greater black-backed gulls, before swinging over the camp and the sands, putting up the oystercatchers again and causing consternation among the kittiwakes, about 100 of which were bathing in the blue-green shallow waters at the head of Village Bay.

Rise up 15m to pick up a sheep track heading south-east, keep away from the cliff edge, in 100m cross the lower remnants of the Oiseval Wall and continue south, losing height to reach the Point of Coll.

POINT OF COLL

At a time when the ownership of the islands was in dispute between the MacLeods of Dunvegan on Skye and the MacDonalds of Clan Ranald, a race was organised between the rivals. It was decided that two boats should make for the island, one rowed by the MacLeods and the other by the MacDonalds, and that the first to touch the island would claim it for his Chief. The race was close and it appeared that the MacDonalds were about to win when a MacLeod chopped off his hand and cast it ashore, thus being the first to touch St Kilda.

Euphemia MacCrimmon told a modified version of the same story in the 1860s to Miss Anne Kennedy: 'There were two brothers, one named Colla Ciotach, the other Gilespeig Og, or Young Archibald. Each of them had a boat, and both were racing to St Kilda, for he who got there first was to be the proprietor. When they neared St Kilda, Coll saw that his brother would arrive there first; so Coll cut off his hand, and threw it on the east point, which the boats pass as they come into the harbour, and cried to his brother, 'This (the hand) is before you'; and the point is called *Gob Cholla*, or Coll's Point to this day; there is a well not far from the point called also *Tobar Cholla*, or Coll's Well.'

The Village and Mullach Mór. The track to the Point of Coll gives splendid views back to the gentle curve of the Village street with the Factor's House, cottages and the slopes of Conachair and Mullach Mór beyond.

This is traditionally the place where, in a westerly wind and an ebb tide, the St Kildans launched their mail boats carrying pleas for help in times of hardship, starvation or shipwreck. These were often picked up on the shores of the Outer Hebrides, others rounded Cape Wrath to land on Birsay or Roussay on Orkney, or drifted on to the Scandinavian coast. Often their message got through. In 1876 Sands, having been marooned on Hirta for several months, obtained an early reply to his letter. It went ashore on Birsay, was delivered to Stromness where the message was telegraphed to London and, within three weeks of sending the letter, he was rescued from St Kilda by HMS *Jackall*.

Children often fished for mullet here after school. It was the place of a tragedy in October 1906 when Norman Gillies, aged 13, slipped and fell from the rocks. The fearful current swept him out to sea before help could reach him and he was last seen clinging to his fishing rod.

Return to the Oiseval Wall and ascend alongside it.

OISEVAL WALL

This extraordinary structure ascends in practically a straight line. It was built to keep cattle from straying down the cliffs of Oiseval. If they wandered down there it was almost impossible to retrieve them – they were more likely to fall to their deaths.

ST KILDANS' 'OISEVAL TRAVERSE'

This is to be considered only by very experienced climbers. The clear sheep track leads away in an easterly direction near the top end of the wall – much higher than you would expect. It slopes steadily down to a rock notch, passes through this, goes round and down again. The path then continues on the level right round Oiseval, coming to

an abrupt end near the Gap where recent rock falls have demolished it. To get out requires a strenuous scramble up a steep grassy cliff face to reach safety. It traverses at about 150m above the sea, is very dangerous and should only be attempted with great care and with the right equipment. It is interesting to observe the routes the St Kildans took!

The eastern extremity of Oiseval ends in *Rubha an Uisge*, headland of the waters, where a stream drops to the sea in a thin waterfall.

Continue to the summit of Oiseval.

OISEVAL SUMMIT (290m, 950ft)

Drink in the view, if the mist isn't enveloping the summit. Anything attempting to survive up here gets a tremendous battering from the wind and rain, and sea spray at certain times. The elements leave their mark on the vegetation and the cleitean, few of which have any soil or grass on their tops. Scoured areas are devoid of soil which simply

Above: Looking towards the Gap from Oiseval an array of cliffs unfold. These are the sites of the St Kildans' perilous climbing exploits to collect the fulmars and their young.

Right: The descent from Conachair affords an excellent view of the enclosures on An Lag, built of massive stones of buff-coloured Conachair granophyre. Some boat-shaped settings can just be picked out.

gets blown off, and many of the plants are stunted in their growth. In contrast, only a few metres away in a little hollow, or some protection given by a rock or cleit, there are comparatively lush pockets.

Plants surviving up here on the summit are also found on Conachair and Mullach Bì, and include the coarse-leaved great woodrush; associated in similar grassland are fine bent, mat grass and sweet vernal grass. On the upper seaward ledges where grazing sheep and salt spray have a greater effect, fine bent and red fescue dominate, lower down, where the vegetation has to survive the guano from the nesting seabirds, common sorrel is one of the few plants to thrive.

Head north-north-west keeping fairly close to the cliff edge and follow it down to the Gap.

THE GAP – BETWEEN OISEVAL AND CONACHAIR

The St Kildans never called this place the Gap but *Bearradh na h-Eige*, pronounced 'beren-ee-haykee' meaning, 'the ridge of the Gap', or 'the cliff of the Gap'. It is a staggering place where the cliff drops vertically for nearly 200m to the sea below and the undercutting caves. Someone was recently led blindfolded up the last 20m from An Lag to a secure position on the edge of the cliff. When the cover was removed the person was absolutely speechless. It is perhaps here that one feels the truth of Sands' words: 'I have said hills, but in reality they are only halves of hills – hills to the interior, cliffs to the sea'.

Fulmars wheel, glide and turn with stiff wings often in a vertical plane skimming the cliff edges as they follow the contours with the backcloth of Boreray and the Stacs. On the perpendicular rock walls other adults or young sit on tiny ledges or little grassy overhangs and rock turrets. Two hundred metres far below, fulmars look like tiny snowflakes, circling round just above the surface of the sea. Occasionally killer whales can be seen through the clear water, hunting one of their favourite prey, the grey Atlantic seals which frequent the huge caves at the foot of the cliffs such as *Geò na Eige*, Cleft Cave, visible from here.

These caves have been formed by erosion following the last igneous activity when black molten dolerite was squeezed under pressure between cracks in the Conachair granite. These black bands and sheets of dolerite cut across the cliffs of Conachair and Oiseval and at sea-level they offered less resistance to the onslaught of the waves so these weaker sections were eroded away. Some of the caves are immense and extend under the cliffs for 75m. Recent rock falls reveal the lovely buff colour of the Conachair granite and have destroyed the end of the St Kildans' Traverse which can be seen from here.

An excellent time to be here is on a clear sunny summer evening when the light on Boreray is golden and the low sun casts wonderful shadows of the pinnacles of *Clagan na Rùsgachan*, right across the grassy south-west face of Boreray and the mass of nesting gannets are illuminated in a glorious way.

Follow the line of cleitean south-west down to An Lag, between the enclosures, through the Head Dyke and back to the Jetty.

Ruaival, Oiseval and the north end of Dùn.
Looking through the Caolas an Dùin from the seaward side gives a magnificent view through to Oiseval, and the remains of the old wall, built to keep cattle from straying down the cliff.

Conachair Walk

Conachair Summit (426m, 1,397ft)
This walk takes in the oldest stone structures in St Kilda on An Lag, the staggering views at the Gap and St Kilda's highest peak, Conachair. Allow four to five hours.

From the Jetty, walk up the main street, past the Factor's House and over the Dry Burn. Turn immediately right before the Blackhouse, just to the east of House No. 1. Walk up the left side of the Dry Burn for about 40m.

The near vertical slopes and rock faces of Conachair plunge nearly 427 metres to the sea below, and form Britain's highest sea-cliffs. The grassy and rocky ledges here provide nest sites for 6,000 pairs of fulmars.

OLD TRACK
The Dry Burn cuts across one of the old tracks just below the Head Dyke. On the right of the burn the army water tanks are built on the track which makes its way down towards the store. This track is also visible to the left (west) of the burn, but it gets lost among the cleitean and enclosures as it heads up towards the old pre-1834 village.

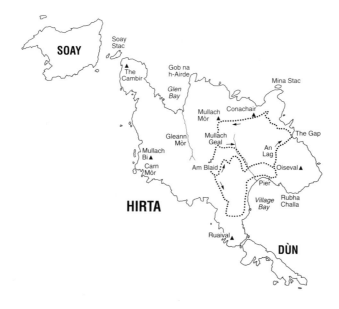

Continue up the left side of the dry burn, through the gap in the Head Dyke and up the steep rise onto An Lag.

AN LAG BHO'N TUATH

'The hollow in the north', An Lag lies between Conachair, the Gap and Oiseval; the bowl has been hollowed and deepened by the action of its own small ice sheet which deposited a little terminal moraine at the village edge. It has been partly filled in, particularly on the south side, by the downward creep of gravel and stone.

When schoolmaster John Ross wrote an account of his time on St Kilda in 1889, on his sketch map he called An Lag *Glen Beag*, the Little Glen, as opposed to *Gleann Mór*, the Great Glen. About 100m above the Head Dyke on the east side of the burn are huge, rough boat-shaped settings, but better ones are close at hand.

BOAT-SHAPED SETTINGS

These ancient monuments are composed of several large stones set on edge, some have one side convex, some have both, all are longer than they are wide and most come to a point at both ends, giving the structure a boat-like appearance. Well over half of each stone is embedded below ground level, and to keep them upright, most of them are 'pegged' with smaller stones. A soil sample sent for carbon dating was found to be approximately 1850 BC. An excellent example is to be found at the top of the rise above the Head Dyke near the first cleit. The setting is 10m to the left; another, less good, is 10m to the north of the same cleit, and there are others in the vicinity.

There are a few cairns on the edge of the level part of An Lag, they are circular piles of stones but are difficult to differentiate from ruined cleitean. Wheatears and St Kilda Wrens frequent this area.

Walk on a further 100m to the centre of the enclosures.

Boat-shaped Setting.
On the ice-hollowed valley on An Lag, just above the Village, several of these structures can be found. They are the earliest monuments on St Kilda. No remains have been found within them and their use is open to discussion.

ENCLOSURES

These enclosures are sometimes called sheep fanks, but they were only used to enclose large numbers of sheep when the hoggs (yearling sheep) were held here prior to being shipped to Dùn for winter. Normally they were kept to provide good grazing for weak lambs or ewes needing nourishment and protection when vulnerable. Each enclosure was owned by one or more of the families for their own use. The walls are 2m high in places and are made with massive chunks of Conachair granite.

Follow through between the enclosures to the line of cleitean.

LINE OF CLEITEAN

These cleitean, and all those up the sides of Oiseval and Conachair, were used to store turf which the St Kildans removed from nearby and dried for fuel. Turf was accessible and convenient to bring down to the village but greatly reduced the quality of the grazing and now, with acid soil and little effect from sea spray, heather has taken over.

Each cleit has lush vegetation around it including a variety of grasses and common chickweed.

Continue up the line of cleitean until the Gap is reached.

FULMAR HARVEST

These sea cliffs at the Gap, right round Conachair, and particularly those at the Cambir, were some of the best for the Fulmar Harvest. It began around 12 August with each family allocated shares of the cliffs. Men would descend these vertical cliffs on ropes, dangling like a spider on a thread, working along ledges until they had killed about 30-40 young. They would tie them into bundles which were then hauled up to the top of the cliff. The women and children then carried them down to the village. Here they would be plucked, gutted and salted for the winter. They apparently tasted like roast pork. About 125 birds would be salted for each inhabitant. Between 1829 and 1929 about 10,000 birds were taken on average each year.

Mullach Bì & the Cambir Walk

This long walk takes in the impressive western and northern cliffs of Hirta, culminating in excellent views across the Sound to Soay. Allow at least six hours.

From the Jetty either walk along the village street, cross Abhainn Mhór, pick up the tarmac road and continue up to the quarry or follow the tarmac road on the coastal side of the meadow, cross Abhainn Mhór and ascend to the quarry.

QUARRY

The quarry did not exist when the island was inhabited, but was opened up to provide bottoming for the road below the meadow up to Mullach Mór and Mullach Sgar. It is a source of interest to geologists as the Mullach Sgar complex is clearly exposed at this point and shows the later intrusions of microgranite, dolerites and microdiorites. It

Looking across from Bioda Mór, the rugged cliffs of Dùn and Ruaival lead up to Mullach Bì in the distance.

follows the last major igneous intrusion of Conachair granophyre which dates back 56 million years.

CLACH A' BHAINNE, MILKING STONE

This massive stone lies 10m to the right of the road and 10m short of the track which branches off just below the quarry giving access to it. In medieval times the custom was to pour out some milk into a hollow in the stone. It was carried out on Sundays in summer and autumn to placate a subordinate divinity called *Gruagach*.

TIGH AN TRIAR, HOUSE OF THE TRINITY

This large cleit is situated 30m from the road on the right-hand side, on the second bend above the quarry among a cluster of cleitean. It is unusual in having a single chamber with two entrances on the south side, now silted up and grassed over.

Clach a' Bhainne, The Milking Stone. A distinctive isolated rock, near the road junction to the quarry, used by the St Kildans in medieval days for their superstitious customs.

Continue up the road, the gradient eases off, another tarmac road comes in from the left from Mullach Sgar. Carry on up the road to the zebra crossing.

AM BLAID, WIDE MOUTH

The broad flat col at just over 210m is Am Blaid, separating Village Bay and Glen Bay. Three routes open up from Am Blaid, where the Mullach Sgar road comes in on the left:

(1) Mullach Mór and Conachair – Follow the tarmac road upwards and northwards.

(2) Gleann Mór – After the junction continue north up the road for 100m, at the third cleit on the left, turn left (west north-west) between a group of cleitean. Follow the track down which passes close to the right side of a line of cleitean.

Continue down the right side (east) of the glen.

(3) Mullach Bì and the Cambir – After the road junction turn left 30m before the next cleit, go in a westerly direction on the track which gradually fades out. Within 200m the earth dyke should be reached. Follow the dyke to the west. If it is not misty, the summit of Mullach Bì should be visible.

EARTH DYKE
The Earth Dyke forms a continuous turf wall round the head of Gleann Mór. It was built to keep the cattle in the Great Glen during the summer, where the grazing was more luxuriant, and to keep them away from the growing crops in the village. The women went over daily to milk the cows and then returned to the village with it.

Tigh an Triar, House of the Trinity. This is an unusually large cleit on the St Kildans' track leading over to the Great Glen. It had a special function when they were transferring their cattle in spring and autumn.

Follow the earth dyke as it curves in a south-west direction, just beyond Cnoc Sgar leave the path and head left to the high rocky headland of Claigeann Mór (Skull Rock), for magnificent views south-east to Ruaival and Dùn. Continue north-west along the high ground at the top of the cliff until the Lover's Stone is reached.

LOVER'S STONE
An earlier writer has led people astray having confused this with the Mistress Stone on Ruaival. The St Kildans certainly never called it the Lover's Stone but by the

impressive Gaelic, *Bearradh na cloiche moire*, pronounced 'Beren a quasha mora', the ridge of the big rock.

CLAIGEANN AN TIGH FAIRE, SKULL OF THE WATCHING HOUSE

From *bearradh na cloiche moire*, and on the ridge below it, the Skull Rock stands out dramatically ahead – complete with furrowed brow, eye sockets, nasal cavity, elongated chin – only a few teeth are missing! It is situated near one of the many watching houses which the St Kildans manned a few centuries ago when they were fearful of pirates and other thieves who frequented the seas.

Keep along the top of the ridge, losing height first before the ridge rises steeply and passes amongst a number of cleitean. The earth wall ends here.

CLEITEAN CLUSTER

Many of the cleitean round here have nesting storm petrels – all through the hours of darkness during the breeding season they pour out their purring song to attract their mates back home. In the 1920s these cleitean were all owned by different families and were used to dry peat. The best peat was found in Gleann Mór where it was dug and carried up in bags to dry in these cleitean. It would dry more quickly here, exposed to the wind, and it was easier to carry the bags along the turf dyke and down to the village during the winter.

CARN MÓR, THE BIG ROCKS

Carn Mór is the great boulder field at the foot of Mullach Bì, formed by huge blocks of gabbro from the mountain above in the Quaternary period. Some of the individual blocks are 7m or more in length.

The St Kildans would come at night in the spring to catch the shearwaters. They would have a trained dog with them to catch the birds as they landed, before they had time to enter their own burrows. Sometimes as many as 60 would be caught in one night. Leach's petrels, storm petrels

Large colonies of puffins are found on St Kilda (over 250,000 in total). Their colourful beaks are multi-purpose, valuable in courtship, fighting, excavating burrows and in catching and holding up to 60 small fish!

and puffins nest here in large numbers.

GEÒ AN EIREANACH, IRISHMAN'S CAVE

At the foot of Mullach Bì at the north end of Carn Mór is Irishman's Cave – the point at which an unfortunate Irishman landed unexpectedly. The inhabitants spotted the wrecked remains of a boat off the rocks opposite this geò and men were lowered on ropes to investigate. They were very surprised to find a man in a weakened state on the rocks. They rescued him and were amazed at his story. He had set off on Christmas Day to row across the bay near his home in his native isle, with a keg of whisky to make merry with his friends. A sudden squall quickly took him out of the protection of the bay and soon he found himself being blown by a series of south-westerlies. He was at the mercy of wind and wave and eventually his rowing boat was smashed up on the rocks – hence 'Irishman's Cave'. It was over a year before he managed to escape from the island and return home.

MULLACH BÌ, PILLAR SUMMIT

Mullach Bì is the highest point on the western cliffs (358m, 1,192ft) and rises majestically above the surrounding coastline giving superb views in all directions and a first view of Soay. There is a marked contrast between this rugged coastline of gabbro and that of the rounded hills of Conachair and Oiseval to the east. The summit is covered with a lush growth of great woodrush.

A little further north, having come off the summit plateau, there is a strange 'peep hole' formed by a narrow gully blocked at the top by a large rock. It appears to be partly natural and partly man-made. It possibly dates back to the times in the past when watchmen were posted to give warning of brigands. It gives a good view down to the lower grassy slopes and the sea far below.

Continue along the cliff edge which gives magnificent views of the rocks and across to Soay. The ridge ends in rough rocky ground where the land falls away steeply, carry on until the neck of the Cambir is reached.

The Lover's Stone.
This huge rock gave the whole ridge its name, 'the ridge of the big rock'. The St Kildans never called it the Lover's Stone, and it should not be confused with their true 'lover's stone' – the Mistress Stone on Ruaival.

POLL A' CHOIRE, KETTLE OR CALDRON BAY

At the narrowest part here, the neck of the Cambir, look west over the cliffs to the well-named bay, especially if there is a rough sea running, *Poll a' Choire*. Some huge slabs of rock protrude out of the sea below and at their base are convenient ledges where large numbers of grey Atlantic seals haul themselves out and laze away their days, singing their mournful songs from time to time.

Keep along the west cliffs which gives good views of rock needles hundreds of metres below, very spectacular in swirling mist!

STACS IN SOAY SOUND

The Sound is only 8m deep at low tide but some 500m of boiling sea separate the island of Soay from Hirta out of which rise three imposing stacs of gabbro. *Stac Biorach*, the Pointed Stac, stands 73m (240ft) in height, and is considered to be the most difficult to climb. In earlier days it was climbed yearly and basketfuls of guillemot eggs were lowered to the boat. Soay Stac stands 61m (200ft) in height, is 300m long and has an archway running through it. Probably the least impressive is Stac Dona (27m, 87ft), known by the St Kildans as 'the Bad Stac' on account of the small number of birds and eggs that could be harvested there. The view of Soay from here is interesting and imposing, the cliffs and the usual landing place; binoculars are needed for *Tigh Dugan*, the Altar and the remains of a crashed World War Two Wellington bomber.

CAMBIR, CRESTED RIDGE

The Cambir rises up like the prow of a ship to a height of 216m (693ft) and forms the north end of Hirta. The near vertical cliffs all round, some with grassy ledges, provide suitable nest sites for thousands of fulmars. Known to the St Kildans as *Han Cambelyer*, it was a long haul for them to carry a load of fulmars back to the village. The St Kildans also had to collect their sheep from here for marking and dipping. The whole community would head out even if individuals only had two or three sheep in the vicinity. On the west side of the Cambir, just below the highest point, was a very special lush grazing area for the sheep. The St Kildans called this part of the cliff *Sooshla*.

Claigeann an Tigh Faire, **Skull of the Watching House.** This is the most realistic of the different skull rocks on St Kilda, situated near one of the look out points. Once spotted along the ridge towards Mullach Bì, the resemblance is uncanny, with nose, eye sockets, chin and teeth.

Follow the cliff eastwards and then head south to the combe above Mol Carn Na Liana, *the shingle beach of the Cairn of the Green Sword. Here there is a large, accessible puffin colony; a pleasant place to sit and watch their activities. Return by the west side of Glen Bay, heading for Am Blaid, either:*
(1) Retrace steps on the west of Gleann Mór keeping below the summit of Mullach Bì but picking up the earth dyke, or
(2) Cross to the east side of the glen, visiting the Amazon's House and other structures in the vicinity, then head up the line of cleitean at the head of the glen. From Am Blaid follow the road down to the Village, or take a diversion via Mullach Sgar, towards Ruiaval and cut down the grassy slope to St Brendan's, and back to the Village.

Gleann Mór Walk

THE GREAT GLEN
In Gleann Mór there are many indications of human activity on both sides of the wide valley. There are 'horned structures', hut circles, cairns, and a circle of stones, also boulder dykes, enclosures, sheilings, wells and lazy-beds. Allow four to five hours.

Above: Gleann Mór's wide scoop and winding river sweep down to Glen Bay. Horned structures are found in the lower reaches on both sides of the glen.

Below: Looking east across the bay, to the 'the Tunnel' – an amazing long natural arch through the headland of Gob na h'Àirde.

At the quarry continue up the road to Am Blaid. After the road junction, continue along the road for 100m. At the third cleit on the left, turn left (west-north-west) between a group of cleitean. Follow the track down as it passes close to the right-hand side of a line of cleitean. Continue down the right side (east) of the glen.

GLEANN MÓR, THE GREAT GLEN
Gleann Mór is a wide 'U' shaped valley which continues underwater into the bay, to some extent gouged out in more recent times by a small glacier. The glen occupies the space between the earliest igneous intrusion of western

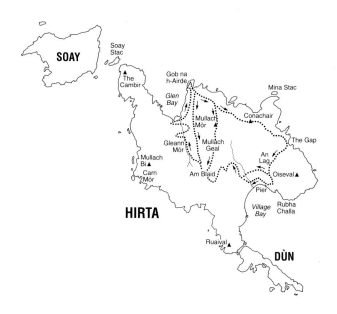

gabbro to the west and the last major intrusion of Conachair granite to the east. All the way down the centre of the Glen is the Mullach Sgar complex with outcrops of granite and gabbro at the northern edge of Glen Bay.

At the head of Gleann Mór, purple moor grass is dominant with bents, red fescue, mat grass, tormentil and sea plantain. There are also cotton grass communities with an increase of heather and two insectivorous plants, the common butterwort and the greater sundew. Areas around the cleitean, the lochans and springs have their own plant communities.

SUNDERLAND FLYING-BOAT REMAINS

Scattered over the glen are pieces of aluminium and other broken bits of metal. They are the remains of a Sunderland flying-boat which was wrecked at the head of the glen in the hour between eleven o'clock and midnight on Wednesday 7 June 1944, the day after D-Day. Twenty tonnes of wreckage now lie mostly underground in the glen, apart from the few pieces remaining on the surface. A plaque in the kirk commemorates the members of the crew who lost their lives in this tragedy.

ABHAINN 'A GHLINNE MHÓIR - THE RIVER OF THE GREAT GLEN

The 'river' rises in a number of small tributaries at the head of the glen. A number of faults cut across the glen in a north-west direction but most of these were covered by deposits from the localised glacier. Lower down there is a kink where the river follows one of these faults before straightening out again. Towards the bay the river falls over a ridge of dolerite and granite before passing over a stretch of granite and then entering Glen Bay.

CIRCLE OF STONES

At about the 100m contour in the curving arm of one of the tributaries, on a flattish patch of grassland to the east of the stream, is a circle of stones. The stones stand only 0.5m in height. Archaeologists tell us that it is a 'circle of stones' rather than a 'stone circle'. It is however unique on St Kilda. Bonxie territory is entered here.

Continue down the 'river' until the tributary emerging from the lochan meets it – follow this up to the lochan.

THE LOCHANS

The lochans, one sizeable and other tiny satellite patches of water, are on the west slope of the glen at about the 100m contour level. Water has collected on a terrace formed by deposits on the edge of the local glacier. Across the glen at the same level a line of springs can be detected indicating that the hill slope deposits have flowed onto the more compacted glacial deposits. The water wells up between the layers in clear springs.

The lochans are favourite places for skuas and gulls to bathe and to dunk their victims.

On higher dryer ground to the west and north of the lochans are six examples of 'horned structures'.

'HORNED STRUCTURES'

There are no records of permanent habitation in Gleann Mór but a total of 20 'horned structures' are to be found in the glen. No similar structures occur in Britain or Europe. They are in two clusters, one on the west of the glen, north and west of the lochans: the other, larger, cluster is to the east of the glen.

They come in different shapes and sizes:

(i) **'Simple horned structures'** – The shape consists basically of a forecourt formed by two horn-shaped walls, which archaeologists consider to have been added at a later date. These lead into a main court (about 3 x 3m) with two or three cells (about 1.2 x 1.6m) branching outwards. The whole structure is made of dry stone, the walls are corbelled and each cell had a covering of turf. The dating of the structures has not been determined but suggestions have varied from the fourth-sixteenth centuries AD.

(ii) **'Complex horned structures'** – These show

91

considerable variation on the same basic plan, some have been developed with a forecourt and two courts with four cells. The most complicated one is near the lochans and has three courts and ten cells. Later generations of St Kildans used them as sheilings in the summer.

Cross the glen to investigate the buildings on the east side, but first look at the springs to the south of the Amazon's house for interesting vegetation.

TAIGH NA BANAGHAISGEICH, FEMALE WARRIOR'S HOUSE – AMAZON'S HOUSE

The east side of the glen had many attractions in terms of habitation as close at hand was a plentiful supply of stones for building material, the slope was well drained and there was a steady supply of spring water available in the vicinity.

Taigh na Banaghaisgeich and its owner featured widely in St Kilda folklore; the stories about her impressed Martin Martin in 1697 but unfortunately he recorded none of them. However, he did describe the house: 'The whole is built of stone without any wood, earth or mortar to cement it, and it is built in the form of a circle pyramidwise towards the top, having a vent in it, the fire always being in the centre of the floor; the stones are long and thin which supplies the defect of wood. The body of this house contains not above nine persons sitting, there are three beds or low vaults that go off the sides of the wall, a pillar betwixt each bed, which contains five men apiece; at the entry of one of these low vaults is a stone standing upon one end fixed; upon this they say she (the Female Warrior) ordinarily laid her helmet: there are two stones on the other side, upon which she is reported to have laid her sword; she is said to have been much addicted to hunting...'

Today the Amazon's House, complex 'F', consists of a large horned forecourt leading into a single court (or fold) with three cells. To this have been added two chambered mounds, and in more recent times three cleitean have been constructed using some of the stones from the mounds.

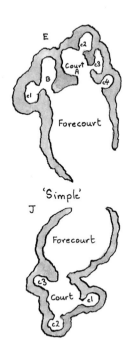

Horned Structures in Gleann Mór.

These ancient structures are found on both sides of the glen. Latterly they were used as summer sheilings where the women attended both cattle and sheep.

'E' Plan shows a Horned structure with a forecourt leading into Court A with three cells and Court B with one. 'E' is the first of these structures going down the east side of the glen.

'J' is a simple structure

OTHER NEARBY STRUCTURES

A great variety of 'horned structures' can be seen in the vicinity, including some splendid examples of simple ones which have been beautifully built and have hardly changed over the years apart from losing the turf covering. Associated with these are boulder dykes and small field enclosures and springs.

TOBAR NAM BUADH, WELL OF VIRTUES

Tobar nam Buadh rises in Gleann Mór close to the Bay. A low substantial stone building with a stone roof covers the spring which forms a pool in the floor of the cell. The water here is refreshing, clear, cool and diuretic! It was believed to possess healing properties and was a favourite place with the St Kildans.

GEÒ NAN RÒN, SEALS' CAVE

At this point the river reaches Glen Bay and grey Atlantic seals abound in the surrounding waters and caves. This is the eastern margin of the Glen Bay granite intrusion which spreads westward.

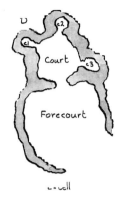

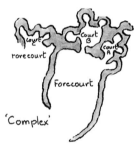

having one forecourt leading to a single court with three cells. This is lower down the glen towards the Well of Virtues.

'D' is another example of a simple structure situated nearer the river.

The 'Complex' horned structure has two forecourts, one leads into Courts A and B, each of which has three cells. The other leads into Court C which also has three cells. This is on the west side of the glen.

Lachlan MacDonald remembered a tragedy here on a misty winter's night with a gale blowing. One of the Fleetwood trawler skippers, well known for his kindness in bringing mail and groceries, trying to find some protection took his boat into the cave. It hit the rocks and sank there with the loss of eight men. The accident must have been sudden; the water is very deep, and although it was a large boat only the tips of the masts were showing at low tide.

LEACAN AN EITHEIR, FLAT BOAT ROCKS

These rocks have been formed by the intrusion of the fine-grained Glen Bay granite. Boats could be hauled up here in calm weather.

GEÒ CHRUADALIAN, HARDSHIP CAVE

This cave receives the outflow of the Abhainn Alltan and was the site of another accident. Divers have found the wreckage of a trawler at about 17m, the boiler, parts of the engine and other bits and pieces still remain on the bottom.

LAZY-BEDS

A little way to the west of Geò Chruadalian is evidence of a small patch of lazy-beds. One of the stewards at the beginning of the 1700s encouraged the St Kildans to try cultivating new areas of ground, turning them over and sowing them. The results were poor and the islanders considered it was best left for grazing.

Retrace your path following the bay eastwards and then take the track north to Gob na h-Àirde.

GOB NA H-ÀIRDE, POINT OF THE HIGH GROUND

On the flat top there are still the remains of some iron stakes put there by the St Kildans. Together with netting from the trawlers they made a temporary sheep fank here for use at clipping time. The sheep were collected and brought from the Cambir and Gleann Mór.

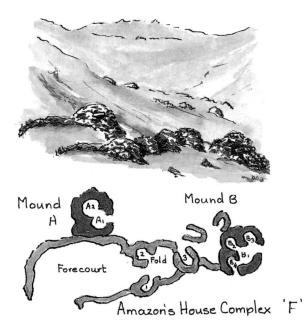

Amazon's House Complex 'F'. This house is featured widely in St Kildan folklore. It was still intact in the 1850s but is deteriorating fast.

Erosion of the softer dolerite sheets under the headland has produced the natural arch (and the one on Soay Stac). A sloping path on the west of the headland leads down to the tunnel; sea spleenwort clings to the rocky sides here. The varied colours are magnificent and occasionally a seal will have hauled itself up onto the rocks for a rest from playing in the raging surf. Puffins are usually swimming nearby on the Glen Bay side of the arch with nesting kittiwakes above and a few razorbills and guillemots on the ledges. A magical place with a wonderful view through the arch to Boreray and the stacs.

Return either by taking the quick route up the glen and down the road to the village, or by following the steep cliff edge, walking south-east to Glacan Mór, and on to Conachair and the Gap, then down An Lag to the Village and the Jetty, or alternatively, at Glacan Mór a shorter route would be to Mullach Mór and then down the road to the village.

Tobar nam Buadh,
Well of Virtues.
This well continually produces clear, fresh water, and is protected by walls and a canopy. It has been a favourite with St Kildans for centuries.

95

The Other Islands

HIRTA'S SATELLITE ISLANDS AND STACS
Island of Dùn
Stac Levenish
Island of Soay
The Stacs in Soay Sound
This section includes the southern outlier, Stac Levenish; the major islands of Dùn to the south and of Soay with its attendant stacs to the north.

These islands and stacs are linked by underwater ridges and are the relics of the southern and western rim of the extinct tertiary volcano. They were too small or inaccessible to be permanently inhabited but most were visited regularly during the year in the round of activities on St Kilda for the harvesting of birds and the management of sheep.

The southern outliers include Stac Levenish, a pyramidal shaped rock, small by St Kildan standards, rarely visited by the inhabitants, and the island of Dùn. Dùn forms the long western arm of the Village Bay protecting it from the Atlantic. This island was visited frequently as a 'great place for puffins' and a useful wintering ground for some of their sheep.

To the north is the island of Soay, separated from the Village by an awkward sea journey. Owing to the turbulent waters and the difficulty in landing and leaving, Soay is reckoned to be the least visited island in Britain. However, many of today's visitors will look across from Hirta to its massive form and others may have the opportunity to sail below its imposing cliffs.

Between Soay and the north point of Hirta three stacs rise up in the Sound of Soay, each quite different in shape and rarely visited by the St Kildans.

Glen Bay, seen from Mullach Mór, is the home of grey Atlantic seals and the site of many wrecked boats. Beyond is the Cambir, the northern headland of Hirta, with the great mass of the Island of Soay behind.

97

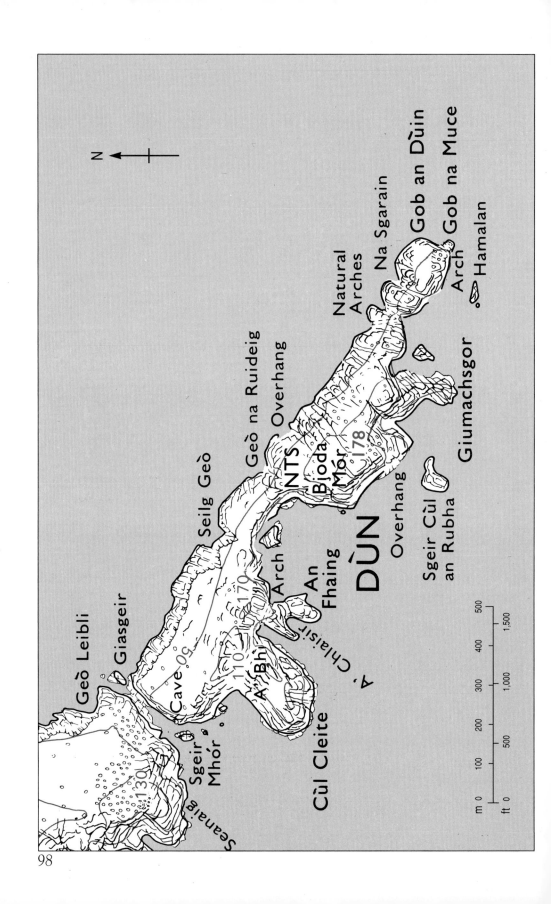

N

Geò Leibli

Giasgeir

Seanaig

Sgeir
Mhór

130

Cave

50

A' Bh

Arch

110

170

A' Chlaisir

Cùl Cleite

Seilg Geò

Geò na Ruideig

Overhang

An
Fhaing

NTS

Bioda
Mór

178

DÙN

Overhang

Sgeir Cùl
an Rubha

Giumachsgor

Natural
Arches

Na Sgarain

Gob an Dùin

Gob na Muce

Arch

Hamalan

m 0   100   200   300   400   500
ft 0   500   1,000   1,500

Dùn

DÙN – FORT (178m, 583ft)

Like Boreray, Dùn is a natural rocky fortress. Towards the
southern end there is a beautifully constructed wall of local
stones with a broad base and parapets inside, which led
some to think that this might have been a hill fort. It is
more likely that the wall was erected to prevent sheep from
wandering onto this grassless, dangerous headland. Sands,
in 1875, was shown the site of an altar, which is marked on
Mathieson's 1928 map, but the stones had already been
removed. At the same time he 'saw a low cavern called
Sean Tigh, Old House, on Dùn, which is sometimes
occupied by the men who go to pluck the sheep, and by
the women who go to that island to catch the birds'.

To anyone who has survived a rough 8 hour crossing
from the Outer Hebrides (or a 22-48 hour voyage from
Oban!) entering Village Bay under the protection of Dùn is
a tremendous relief. After the incessant pitching and
tossing like a cork in the ocean, the calm waters bring
immediate comfort in more ways than one. Without the
breakwater of Dùn it is unlikely that St Kilda would have
been inhabited for any length of time. However, it gives no
protection when the wind rises in the east or from the
terrific downdrafts which suddenly and dramatically surge
from the slopes of Conachair, whipping up the surface of
Village Bay. To be caught unawares in Village Bay when an
easterly rises can double the time of the return voyage back
to the security of the Outer Hebrides – 16 hours is an
uncomfortably long ride against wind and tide!

**Before landing and exploring Dùn, the Warden
should be consulted about suitable routes in order to
avoid unnecessary damage and disturbance to the
colonies of birds which are being carefully monitored.
Allow at least two hours.**

Bioda Mór (left), where fulmars glide and wheel and puffins fly past on great aerial pathways. A marvellous viewpoint for the southern half of St Kilda. Thrusting skyward, the sculpted rock of An Fhaing and Cùl Cleite (above) are riddled with caves underneath, providing nesting sites for hundreds of razorbills, guillemots and kittiwakes.

the perpendicular cliff assisted by a long chain which still remains today. At other times they landed from the boat on the rocks at the north-east end of the island to catch birds or to pluck the sheep, although in this century they used Dùn mainly for wintering the hoggs and the rams.

They would come, in the olden days, in March to hunt guillemots by night. A man would be lowered onto a suitable ledge, wearing a white towel on his shoulders. The returning guillemots thought they were landing on a guano covered ledge only to be grabbed, killed and placed on the ledge at his feet. One man could catch 600 in a single night.

Dùn was a favourite place for catching fulmars and puffins for their feathers and nutritional value. Some puffins were caught by reaching them in their burrows, others with sliding horsehair nooses. Roasted by the fire they made a 'nice wee snack'. Sands wrote, 'At that time the few people left in the village were also busy plucking feathers; and the smell of roasted puffins – "a very ancient and fish-like smell" – came from every door... I ate a puffin by way of experiment, and found it tasted like a kippered herring, with a flavour of the dogfish. Custom would no doubt make it more palatable.' (Sands, 1877.)

NESTING SEABIRDS

Remarkable numbers of sea-birds nest on Dùn – with unknown numbers of Manx shearwaters (which can be heard during 'anchor watch' on a boat at night) and storm and Leach's petrels. The recent counts show:-

Puffins	41,600 occupied burrows (55-60,000 in 1975)
Fulmars	12,018 nest sites occupied
Guillemots	2,648 individuals
Razorbills	1,809 individuals, with the largest concentration of about 1,000 at the southern end
Kittiwakes	1,231 occupied sites
Shags	21 nests
Black Guillemots	10 individuals
Great Black-backs	12 territories
Lesser Black-backs	13 territories
Herring Gull	4 territories

DÙN SUMMIT

Richard Castro, leader of several NTS work parties, told me of an experience of his when he visited Dùn: 'I could see that the puffin slopes ahead were strangely empty. As I struck up towards the summit I became aware of a great commotion of birds wheeling over the colony and out across the western cliffs in a busy confused merry-go-round. I made my way to the top, carefully avoiding the wobbly tussocks between burrows, and collapsed on the soft dry summit grass. From my perch I could see the birds circling out over the Atlantic and also the cause of their concern. Teams of big hungry black-backed bullies were patrolling the slopes awaiting opportunities to swoop down and pick up a puffin.

'Lying back in the warm sunshine thinking how lucky

I was to be there I was suddenly startled by the whir of wings close by as a puffin flew very low over me. More and more birds loomed out of the blue, coming in from the sea and rising over the summit. Because of their flight path they couldn't see me until they were right over me, only feet above my head. They were mostly puffins, but also guillemots and razorbills busily beating along with big paddles splayed out behind. They appeared quite startled to see me lying there, they cocked their heads, and looked me straight in the eye. Occasionally a fulmar would gracefully glide over. Some of the auks carried beakfuls of goodies plucked from the sea but none was startled enough to drop its fish supper into my lap. Avoiding the marauding gulls, they would deliver them to their burrow-bound young.'

Sometimes Dùn is strangely quiet with only a few puffins to be seen – all the rest are either incubating eggs in the burrow or feeding out at sea. At other times the air is swarming with thousands of flighting puffins, often racing round and round the island. In August fledgling puffins, deserted by their parents, emerge from the burrows under cover of darkness and make their way down to the sea. Here they are attracted by the lights of the generators and make their way over to the army camp where they are collected up by the Warden and his helpers, weighed, measured and released into the sea just before dawn.

Island of Dùn. The rugged Dùn skyline as seen from the Village, together with its caves and tunnels. It protects Village Bay from the onslaught of the sea providing the wind is not easterly.

Levenish

STAC LEVENISH – STREAM, TORRENT (62m, 203ft)

Stac Levenish, which guards the entrance to Village Bay, can be seen from at least 30 miles away in clear conditions. It rises like a blunt precipitous pyramid, 2.4km (1.5 miles) east of Dùn, to which it is connected by an underwater ridge, part of the rim of an extinct volcano. To a lesser extent the rim continues round and links with Boreray and then on to Soay and Hirta. Heathcote (1900) commented, 'the rocks are very firm and there are no loose stones, as during the winter gales the sea washes right over the stack and clears away everything except the solid rock.'

Waves can be seen breaking and exploding as they hit *Na Bodhan*, the Submerged Rocks, on the eastern side of Levenish. The currents around the stac are extremely hazardous as the rock thrusts upwards from the Atlantic, receiving no protection at all from wind or waves from any direction of the compass. After a rough and misty crossing, the Kearton brothers in 1896, reported that one of the sailors had called out, ' "Land ahead" – The sight was sublime, in front of us loomed a gigantic rock with its summit buried in white mists, and its base surrounded by a fringe of foam left by the broken billows.'

The rock is too small to have a sheltered side and it is difficult to land even in calm weather, for low tide reveals a thick fringe of kelp clinging to its base. Smooth slabs rise to about 20m and give way to a series of flat rock terraces just below the vegetation on the summit.

An underwater tunnel runs right through the island with a cauldron of turbulent water in the centre.

Stac Levenish stands guard at the entrance to Village Bay.

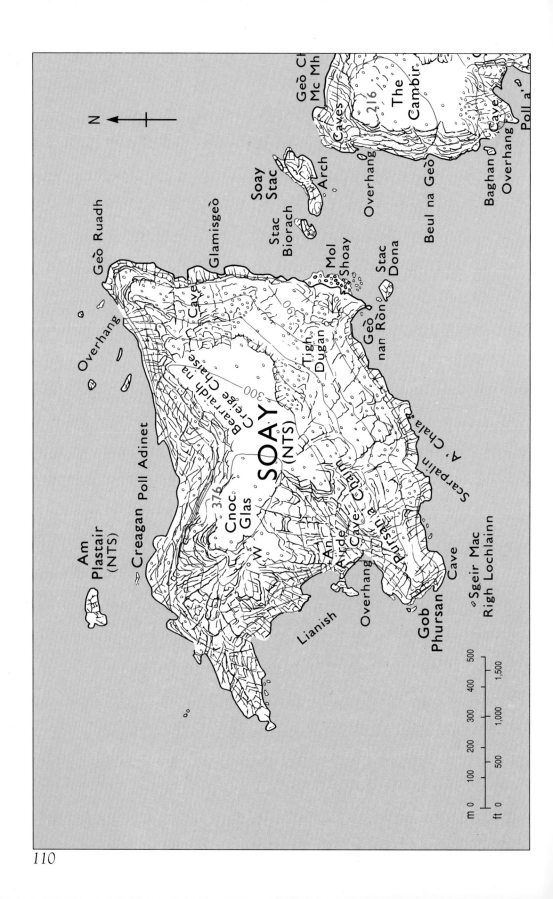

N

Geò Ch...
Mc Mh...

The Cambir

Poll a'

Caves

Overhang

Baghan
Cave
Overhang

216

Beul na Geò

Overhang

Soay
Stac

Stac
Biorach

Arch

Geò Ruadh

Overhang

Glamisgeò

Cave

Mol
Shoay

Stac
Dona

Geò
nan Ròn

090

Tigh
Dugan

A' Chaia

Sgarpalin

300

SOAY
(NTS)

376

Barraidh na
Creige Chaise

Cnoc
Glas

Am
Plastair
(NTS)

Creagan Poll Adinet

Overhang

An
Aird e
Cave

Cave Gian

Purscan

Lianish

Overhang

Cave

Gob
Phursan

Sgeir Mac
Righ Lochlainn
Cave

m 0   100 200 300 400 500
ft 0   500   1,000   1,500

Soay & the Stacs

ISLAND OF SOAY AND THE STACS IN SOAY SOUND

It is difficult to set foot on the Island of Soay. The St Kildans made several visits during the year but they were adept at judging the weather patterns and were extremely skilled in controlling their boats in rough seas at the base of a rugged cliff. But even they got into trouble here on several occasions. Part of the problem is the rapidity with which the weather changes. Within half to one hour conditions may have altered from a calm sea and blue sky with little wind, to a freshening wind with thickening cloud and rough sea. There is no anchorage or suitable place to tie up to the rocks. A back-up boat is essential and anyone landing needs to be alert to the changes in the local conditions and be prepared to adjust their plans to the changing weather patterns and be able to communicate with the boat.

The stacs in Soay Sound are rarely visited. Stac Dona is just a small rock with no nesting birds; Stac Soay is a fantastic shape with a hole gouged right through it, and Stac Biorach is almost inaccessible. Even the St Kildans stopped climbing it around 1840.

Soay

SOAY – 'SHEEP ISLAND' (376m, 1,239ft)

The Vikings named the island *Soay*, Sheep Island, probably because of the strange sheep which they brought or found there. The St Kildans visited the island regularly as it provided fulmars for food, puffins for their feathers and the Soay sheep which they could purchase from the owner. They built bothies and lean-to buildings using the huge rocks and rockfaces, as well as walls to channel the sheep into a defile where they could then be cornered and caught. There is a well, without a canopy, to the west of the summit, Tobar Ruadh, a pool of water surrounded by a circle of stones and vegetation.

Peter Moore, the Warden on St Kilda at the end of the 1980s, is one of the few people who have visited Soay for any length of time. He was engaged in research into bird populations and in assisting archaeologists. He was there in poor weather, and the wet conditions under foot made exploring very difficult. He emphasised to me the great dangers in staying on Soay and other outlying islands due to the difficult terrain, and the problems of getting on and off which can be hazardous as the weather changes so quickly and the conditions can become wet. He remarks: 'The scale of Soay is vast, the perception of the island from across Soay Sound does little to prepare anyone for the enormous boulders, long slopes and difficult terrain that one must traverse in an exploration of the island. Because of the effort involved in making height from one of the landing places to what may be considered a relatively safe foothold, one is acutely aware of the threatening terrain and isolation of Soay at all times.'

A good profile of the great mass of Soay is obtained from the Mullach Bì ridge on Hirta looking across Soay Sound. Among the boulders above is Tigh Dugan and the

St Kilda lies on the path of Atlantic storm belts. Sunset, rain and cloud come in quick succession from the west across Soay, seen here from Mullach Bì.

remains of the Wellington bomber which crashed during World War Two.

Circumnavigation of the island in a small boat reinforces Peter's description. Mol Shoay, Soay's shingle beach, is made up of huge boulders where the grey Atlantic seals haul themselves out to have their pups in October and November. Forbidding perpendicular cliffs arise at the back of the beach. Heading northwards note the impressive overhanging cliffs and the jaws of *Glamisgeò*, Vice-like Cave, before the north-east headland is reached with its *Geò Ruadh*, Red Cave. John Reid informs me that, 'recently the divers have named one of the rocks off this north-east corner of Soay, *Sgeir Fosgailte*, Open Rock; far below the surface it is in the form of a beautiful hollow shell. At a depth of 48 metres you find the only patch of sand, quite small, surrounded by boulders the size of tv sets. You look towards the rock where you can see an obvious opening, stick your head inside this 3m high arch, look up inside the rock which is absolutely hollow and dark – gin clear! From here you can see two main exits which rise towards Soay. Animal life is just mind blowing – the colours are incredible.'

The whole of the northern wall is imposing with 305m (1,000ft) cliffs and grassy slopes and ledges. Nobody now knows who Adinet was, who gave his name to this bay, *Poll Adinet* and to his unlikely landing place, *Laimhrig Adinet*. However, the St Kildans did land here to collect fulmars working from sea-level up to the lower ledges. Westward, between *Creagan*, Rocks, on Soay and the strange shaped sea-stac, Am Plastair, a fast tide race is often encountered which, coupled with a big swell, can make boating rather hazardous.

Below *Am Plastair*, if Scandinavian, the Blue Post or Blue Stac, otherwise, Place of Splashing, is an underwater cleft running right through the rock. The entrance on the north is 24m high and 15m wide narrowing to 8 by 4m just below the surface to the south. At 40m there is a line of

Tigh Dugan, Soay.
Dugan's House gave some protection from the elements. This exiled sheep stealer from Harris was deposited on Soay to end his days. He excavated a space under a huge slab of rock and built up a wall in front. His bones were later found here!

boulders just like a street of houses. Divers report being amazed at the beauty and grandeur of the place – the blaze of colour, endless caves and crannies, ravines full of saithe with crawfish, lobsters and nudibranchs everywhere.

From the north wall the entire western face of Soay is a series of rock ridges interspersed with grassy spurs and ledges which give way to the incredible knife-edge ridge at *Gob a' Ghaill*, Headland of the Strangers. It is possible to land on a rock ledge at the southern edge of Gob a' Ghaill which is the most westerly point of Soay. The strangers could be Vikings or the English! Between this headland and *Gob Phursan*, Buttress Point, is *Lianish*, Headland of the Slope, and *Gob na h-Àirde*, Headland of the Promontory, a vertical narrow cliff dropping nearly 300m into the sea.

Eating into Gob Phursan is the cave and rising above it *Pursan a' Chaim*, Buttress of the Crooked Ridge. Off this south-west headland is a tiny rock, *Sgeir Mac Rìgh Lochlainn*, Skerry of the Son of the King of Norway, who, in the St Kilda legends, receives unusually rough treatment at the hands of the natives – he is killed while having a drink at a well in Gleann Mór. *Scarpalin*, Sharp Pointed Rock juts out from the southern face of Soay. Beyond this a possible landing place at *A' Chala*, literally harbour, but in fact only a few narrow ledges on a very steep rocky slope give access to the grass above.

Soay from the north. This view from the sea is dominated by the sheer north wall of Soay and the knife-edge ridge of Gob a' Ghaill. On the southern side, where the ridge meets the sea is the 'Strangers' Landing Place'.

At the south-east corner of the island is the normally recognised landing place of Laimhrig na Sròine. Tucked in behind this is Geò nan Ròn and cutting under the landing ridge the cave continues for about 50m and has a link exit with Mol Shoay where some of the boulders are the size of a house. Geò nan Ròn is still frequented by many grey Atlantic seals, the current resident St Kilda population of which is estimated at 3-400. A visitor to the islands in 1799 described the risky method of catching them in Geò nan Ròn on Soay: 'There is a remarkable creek resorted to by a vast number of seals. The method of destroying them is as follows. The natives approach the mouth of it which is very narrow, in one of their boats with as little noise as possible and leaving the boat at the mouth, they rush in with large clubs with which they knock down the seals. They, however, sometimes perish themselves in the attempt, for as they never make the attempt except when the wind is easterly, so if the wind happens to change before they retire, the sea rolls into the creek with such violence that the boat and all in her inevitably perish. They used formerly to pay a considerable part of their rent in the skins of these animals, which however, are not found in such numbers now.'

LANDING AND LEAVING

Seton Gordon, who landed on Soay in 1928, described his experience: 'When it came to my turn to make the leap a rope was passed round beneath my arms and I was dragged ignominiously up the smooth seaweed-covered rocks, so quickly that I had no chance of finding any foothold during the ascent.'

Sands, who was marooned on Hirta in 1876, described his visit to Soay on 14th August: 'I went in the morning with a party of men in a small boat to the islet of Soay. It is exceedingly difficult to land on that small island in any weather, from the swell of the sea and the steepness of the shore; but I determined to go to the top. We landed on the south side. With the end of a rope round my waist, the other end being held by a man on the shore, I leaped

Soay from Mullach Mór at sunset. As the evening flights of puffins draw to a close, Manx shearwaters at the foot of the cliffs prepare to return to their nest burrows under cover of darkness.

on the rocks and climbed up the cliffs at the base, assisted by a pull when needful from a man, who now preceded me. At a short distance up, the rocks became less regular. Great masses of stone spring tower-like out of the ground, and blocks of all sizes are crowded together on the steep acclivity. An old man called MacRuaridh, or the son of Rory, acts as my guide; although he totters on level ground, he goes up the hill without any difficulty. About half way up, amongst masses of huge blocks of stone, he shows me an old house which tradition says was made by one Duncan in ancient times.'

The same writer shared his experiences on leaving: 'Having caught as many fulmars as he could carry, we descended to the rocks where we had landed. The sea had risen considerably since that time. After waiting for about two hours, the boat came round the island heavily laden with fulmars. Some of the crew (there were twelve in all) had got into her on the other side. But four or five came down the rocks to where I was, and cast anxious looks at the boat and the waves, that came sweeping from the west at a right angle with the shore. Two young men sat on the top of the cliff, each holding a rope, by the help of which the others slid into the boat. Then came my turn. A line was fastened round my waist, and a hair rope put into my hand. I was peremptorily requested to take off my shoes; and as I descended, I pushed my toes into any crevice or cranny that offered, until the rock became so smooth that I could find no hold for my feet. Then I was obliged to be passive, and allowed myself to be lowered like a sack until I reached a small limpet-covered shelf on which the waves rose about knee-deep. "Jump! Jump!" shout the crew; and when the boat mounts on the wave, I leap, and fall in a heap amongst the fulmars – all right. The air was quite calm, but the sea continued to rise, and the boat was in imminent danger of being dashed to pieces against the wall...'

TIGH DUGAN, DUNCAN'S HOUSE
This was the home of one of the sheep stealing brothers from Lewis, duly banished to Soay after his dastardly deeds on Hirta. Sands visited the primitive dwelling and having mentioned Dugan, he described his house: 'He took shelter under a huge stone that springs out of the ground like the chisel of a plane. He deepened the floor with his dirk, and built dry stone walls at the sides and front, leaving a door of about 2ft square. Here his dirk and bones were discovered after a time. This primitive hut is surrounded by great masses of huge stones, not easily distinguishable. There are some other primitive houses on the island.'

NESTING BIRDS
Peter Moore, who visited Soay in 1989, speaking of the puffins observed, 'there were about 39,000 burrows occupied out of a total of about 68,000 at the time of the study. In a good year, numbers will be up towards the 68,000 mark and there is suitable turf available for new and additional excavation. Other population figures of note include: (minimum figures) 13 pairs of wrens and 17 pairs

of great skuas, 2 hooded crow nests and 1 raven and a minimum of 6 snipe territories on the summit plateau.' Shags, fulmars, guillemots, razorbills and kittiwakes also nest in large numbers, many in the rocks and beach of Mol Shoay. He suspects that the numbers of shearwaters and petrels in the boulder-field on Soay must be greater than in the comparable colony on Carn Mór on Hirta.

SOAY SHEEP, *Ovis aries*

On Soay there are about 200 of this breed of primitive wild sheep, related to the Mouflon of Sardinia, and possibly introduced to Britain by neolithic farmers; both sexes can have horns, and their coat colour varies from light to dark brown to black. They are remarkably resilient having lived untended by man for many centuries on this exposed rocky islet, often grazing along narrow ledges of the 1,000ft precipices. They belonged to the owner of the island group, but the St Kildans were allowed to take as many as they liked provided they paid for them. Collecting them was no easy matter. The St Kildans would come with their dogs whose fangs were previously broken to prevent damaging the sheep when they had been caught or cornered. This exciting exercise involved running the sheep down one at a time – they called it *Ruagadh*, the chase.

Altar on Soay. This finely built altar has stood for centuries in a commanding position on the summit plateau above the middle of the south-east cliff. The view is stunning – seen here with cloud forming over Mullach Bì and streaming across Mullach Mór and Conachair.

Stacs in Soay Sound

Stac Dona (27m, 87ft) has very rarely been climbed, even when the St Kildans inhabited the islands, simply because there were very few birds to be harvested. This is why it is called *Stac Dona*, the Bad Stac.

Soay Stac (61m, 200ft) was climbed in 1902 by Wigglesworth, a physician and keen ornithologist: 'The rocks here for the first 20 feet or so were pretty perpendicular, but when this portion was surmounted the rest of the climb was quite easy. Owing to the stormy weather which had lately prevailed, the natives had been unable to effect a landing on this Stack that season, previous to my visit, and so the birds had been undisturbed. My stay on the Stack was somewhat curtailed owing to a break in the weather and the setting in of steady rain. The descent was a very different business to the ascent, as the rain had made the rocks so slippery that progression was by no means an easy matter. It looked very much as if we should have to adopt the last resort of the St Kildans, and to take to the water and be hauled through the surf to the boat. At length, however, a favourable opportunity for a jump occurring, I landed safely in the boat, after a drop of about 6 feet, and the other men followed suit as soon as a chance presented itself. This was the most difficult re-embarkation I had all the time I was on St Kilda.'

Richard M. Barrington is the only non-St Kildan to have scaled *Stac Biorach*, Pointed Stac (73m, 240ft), which required the ultimate in climbing skills – even by St Kildan standards. He climbed it in 1883 with the help of Donald MacDonald, the father of Lachlan MacDonald, and Donald MacQueen. Barrington considered it the most dangerous climb he ever undertook although he had been to the top of most of the Alpine peaks. As a test of nerve and agility it is not easy to find its equal.

The steeple-like Stac Biorach points skyward, with Stac Soay to the left.

121

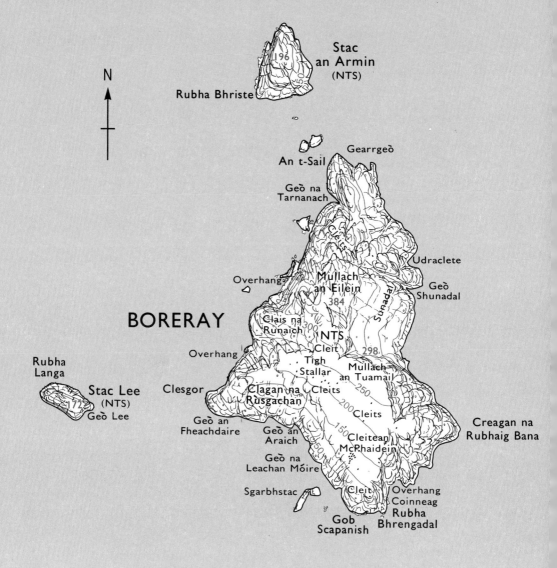

N

Stac
an Armin
(NTS)

Rubha Bhriste
196

Gearrgeò

An t-Sail

Geò na
Tarnanach

Udraclete

Overhang

Cleits

Mullach
an Eilein
384

Geò
Shunadal

BORERAY

Clais na
Runaich

300

Sunadal

NTS
Cleit

298

Overhang

Tigh
Stallar

Mullach
an Tuamal

Rubha
Langa

Clesgor

Clagan na
Rusgachan

Cleits

250

Stac Lee
(NTS)
Geò Lee

172

Cleits

200

Creagan na
Rubhaig Bana

Geò an
Fheachdaire

Geò an
Araich

150

Cleitean
McPhaidein

Geò na
Leachan Mòire

50

Sgarbhstac

Cleit

Overhang
Coinneag
Rubha
Bhrengadal

Gob
Scapanish

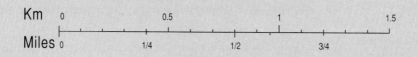

Km   0   0.5   1   1.5

Miles 0   1/4   1/2   3/4

Boreray & the Stacs

ISLAND OF BORERAY
STAC LEE
STAC AN ARMIN

It was the dream of every boy born on St Kilda to join the party going to Boreray and the Stacs. Usually their first opportunity was in the summer time on a visit of 7-10 days to shear the sheep. With no real fuel supply and no anchorage it is unlikely that Boreray could have been occupied for any length of time.

Boreray and its adjacent stacs lie more than 7.5km (4 miles) north-east of Hirta and rise almost vertically out of the sea, from the rim of the extinct volcano on the opposite side from Hirta. They form the site of the largest gannetry in the world with around 50,000 nesting pairs.

It has taken some 50 million years of faulting and weathering to sculpture the rocks into their present shape from the original magma. The continuous onslaught of the relentless sea, the driving rain and the frost have clawed away at the basic volcanic structure causing extensive rock falls and the formation of many new sea-caves and sea-stacs. The process continues today, creating the finest sea-cliff scenery in Britain.

Landing on this very special nature reserve is a rare privilege and permission from the warden on Hirta must be obtained first. Such landing requires particularly passive sea conditions, a cooperative skipper and crew, and an acute awareness of possible changes in the tide and weather conditions. Strong winds can arise within half an hour, unforecasted! Contact with the boat is vital.

Boreray

THE FORTIFIED ISLE (384m, 1259ft)

The island is protected by its spectacular cliffs surmounted by irregularly shaped pinnacles, turrets and towers. There are few places where access may be achieved. The St Kildans used a metal bolt which had been driven into the rock to assist them to land – it has now eroded away.

The St Kildans pronounced the name *Boyra*. Sometimes they called it the 'North Isle', visiting it regularly at night in March and April to collect adult gannets, in May for eggs, in the summer for attending the sheep and lambs and then in September and October to harvest the young gannets or *gugas*, 'fat fellows'. In rough weather they often sheltered in their boats in the huge sea-caves or spent the night there when they were on their fishing expeditions. They would bait and lay the long lines before sleeping in the cave, returning to haul in the catch in the morning.

Today divers speak of unforgetable experiences diving off and under *Sgarbhstac*, Cormorant Rock. John Reid commented, 'The stac itself above water is hardly a stac at all, just a lump of rock, but underwater it can be magical. The visibility has to be at its best – then it is an excellent dive. You can sit on the bottom at 51m and see the top of the arch at 26m – you can see both sides of the large black arch; when the sun is on the arch and there is little plankton to filter the light, there is a beautiful blueness in the water.' Gordon Ridley, author, diver and underwater photographer, reported that the arch is 30m long and 20m wide, seals swim through it and puffins often accompany the divers, the walls are lined with sponge, tubilaria and anemones and at the top of the arch are pockets of glistening exhaled air. The visibility is often about 40m.

Boreray makes its own weather; the rising air cools and condenses to form mist on its western buttresses.

BORERAY LANDING SITE – BELOW THE CLEIT VILLAGE

This is the best landing place, it was used regularly by the St Kildans when they came over to collect gannets and to shear the sheep. It gives easy access up to the Cleit Village and the rest of the island and causes no disturbance to nesting birds.

The site is below the Cleit Village on the sloping slabs east of *Geò Sgarbstac*, Cormorant Rock Cave. There are a number of possible landing rocks here. The sloping slabs are difficult if there is any swell. About 100m to the right are some vertical ledges which are easier to step onto in a swell but, having climbed up the initial 20m of near vertical rock with good footholds, the 'bad step' has to be tackled in order to cross a tricky gully to the left – a definite obstacle to those without climbing experience.

OTHER LANDING SITES

Other sites have been used but these are not recommended as they cause disturbance to the birds or are dangerous owing to slippery conditions or difficult rock faces.

1. Below Clagan na Rùsgachan, is *Geò an Araich*, Cave of Ruin, perhaps the site of some early tragedy or where the St Kildans' boat was lost leaving the men stranded throughout the winter. Landing is on a small ledge of rock to the side of the geo. A rope is necessary to negotiate the initial vertical rock. After this the going is safe ascending the very steep grassy incline but causes considerable disturbance in one of the largest puffin colonies.

2. At *Coineag*, Frothy Bay. To reach this bay pass round the southern tip of Boreray, rounding *Gob Scapanish*, Ness of the Caves, passing *Laimhail*, from *làmh*, 'hand', where huge knuckles of rock reach out into the sea with small caves between, and *Rubha Bhrengadal*, Rounded Headland. Some visitors have used Coineag when the swell has been bad on the western rocks. However, rock climbing experience is strongly advised: this precipitous route requires a good 'head for heights' as a ledge 1m wide has to be crossed with a 30m drop to the sea below!

Gannet. The largest Gannetry in the world is on St Kilda – 50-60,000 pairs. The adults have brilliant white plumage with black wing tips and a strengthened skull. They catch herring and mackerel by plunge diving from as high as 30m. Sometimes they fish near the stacs; other parties are seen 50-70 miles away in the Sound of Harris and beyond.

3. The foot of Mullach an Tuamail is a possible landing place when there is a considerable swell to the west. First pass *Creagan Fharspeig*, Rock of the Greater Black-backed Gull, and the gannet nest site at *Creagan na Rubhaig Bàna*, Rock of the Little White Headland. The landing is suitable only if several hours are available. It is about 100m to the right of some horizontal gannet ledges situated 25m above the sea. The St Kildans landed here with their dogs as it gave access to the grazing sheep and *Sunadal*, South or Sunny Dale, pronounced 'soonatow' by the St Kildans. When they went in the autumn the dogs would catch and hold the sheep which were then killed on the spot and taken back for salting and storage as winter food.

A little snout of rock to the south of a small geo provides a landing point, and a tricky section of the climb follows over slippery rock and vegetation. This leads up into the long steep ascent of Sunadal where the grassy slopes provide nest burrows for 17,000 pairs of puffins and the best sheep grazing area on Boreray. It is an extremely steep valley, mainly facing south and bounded by rock bands and towers. From the boat the prospect is awe inspiring – looking up to *Mullach an Tuamail*, Moundy or Snout Summit (303m, 1,000ft).

EXPLORING THE ISLAND

Allow at least two hours. If the St Kildan landing place near Geò Sgarbhstac has been used, walk up the steep incline to the cleit village 120-140m above the sea.

Cloud cap over Stac Lee, Stac an Armin and Boreray. This day started like the previous one, blue sky and light wind all day with a similar forecast. Within one hour the whole scene had changed, the wind had freshened bringing cloud quickly in from the north and completely enveloping Boreray and the Stacs.

CLEITEAN MCPHAIDEIN, MCFADYEAN'S CLEITEAN – THE CLEIT VILLAGE

In Martin Martin's day, 1697, these cleitean were used to store the harvest of gannets, but later generations kept turf in them for the fires. Leach's petrels nest in them today. Above the cleitean is a small well. On the ridge nearby the St Kildans would remove patches of turf to communicate with Hirta where a watch was kept from the top of the cliffs throughout the period the men were away from home. A piece of turf removed from the southern slope meant their work was finished and they were ready to return, one removed from the left meant they were short of food, one to the right meant injury or death. Occasionally gannets removed turf for nesting material and caused considerable confusion.

This vantage point gives spectacular views of the cleitean in the foreground and Stac Lee rising like a fang from the sea.

Continue due north on the rising path, to the left are the bothy ruins.

THREE BOTHIES

To the left of the path are the ruins of three bothies built into the hillside, only one has the protecting earth wall still standing but each bothy had a single room (4 x 2 x 2m, 12 x 5 x 5ft). These were used by the men collecting gannets or attending the sheep, and by the women who came over to catch puffins. They brought with them a burning peat in a pot, their bedding and their fowling rods, a creel-like basket with enough food for their time on the island, and some extra in case of emergencies.

In 1988 Lachlan MacDonald recalled staying here when he came over to clip the sheep in the 1920s: 'I preferred the top house, furthest away from the landing. The puffins would make an awful mess of the houses... Inside, left of the door, we had the fire; we cut our own peats when we were there and put them in the cleits (we didn't call it a cleit village), ready for next year when we

The great bulk of Boreray has changed its familiar shape, approached here from the south by sea.

would be over again. We took little sticks for kindling and paper for lighting the fire – you needed the fire for cooking. You took a box of food with you for the week or two – meat, oatcakes and scones. You could sleep four on a raised platform built into the hillside, where you also kept all your belongings. We took straw for bedding. You'd be lying on straw and you'd have a blanket over you. You would be quite warm in those houses – there would be some dampness in them when you first went over there. That was no bother in those days.'

Lachlan continued, 'When you had finished your work you would dig a patch of turf to the right of the houses, not by the houses or the cleits but up on the ridge of Boyra, as a signal that you were ready to be collected. It was a large piece of turf you would remove (about 4 x 4m, 12 x 12ft) so it could be seen from Oiseval.'

Donald Gillies was over in Boreray in June 1922 tending sheep when he died from appendicitis aged 36. He was from house No. 14 on Hirta.

TIGH STALLAR, STALLAR'S OR STEWARD'S HOUSE

Sadly, today only a green mound, a cleit and a few stones mark the site of what must have been a most impressive underground house, similar to those on North Rona. Dean Monro who travelled through the Western Isles in 1549 reported: 'The inhabitants have a tradition that it was built by one Stallir, a devout hermit of St Kilda; and had he indeed travelled the universe he could scarcely have found a more solitary place for a monastic life.' Martin Martin saw it in 1697 and said, 'It is much larger than the Female Warriors house in St Kilda, but of the same model in all respects – it is all green without – like a little hill.'

Kenneth Macaulay, who thought that Stallir meant 'man of the rocks', recorded an incident which happened on 6 October 1759. Ten men were landed on Boreray, but the crew of nine could not return to Hirta because of a storm, nor could they land. Eventually, after attempting to shelter under the lee side of one of the stacs, cold and starved, they made a dash for Village Bay. Here three men were washed away and their boat was smashed to pieces on the rocks. Those who had landed on Boreray were marooned there until June of the next year when they were relieved by the Steward, 'without sustaining any great loss, other than being much out of humour.' Assisting their survival were the available birds, sheep, and turf for a fire and the use of Tigh Stallar, which, according to Macaulay,

Boreray – east face.
The ledges on the sheer cliffs are used by thousands of gannets and kittiwakes. Sunadal, a steep grassy 'dale', provides the best grazing for Blackface-Cheviot-cross sheep on Boreray. Left to right: Rubha Brengadal, Creagan Fharspeig, Creagan na Rubhaig Bàna, Mullach an Tuamail, Sunadal, Mullach an Eilein (summit), Geò Sunadal, An t-Sail, Udraclete, Stac an Armin.

'afforded them a very comfortable habitation. Here they slept securely all night and loitered away the whole winter season... On the return of the wild fowl in March, after having relieved their own necessities, they laid up in their store-house a cargo of these, sufficient to load the steward's eight-oared boat.'

Internally, according to Euphemia MacCrimmon who had visited it, 'There were six croops or beds in the wall, one of them very large, called *Rastalla*, the leading climber's cabin; it would accommodate 20 men or more to sleep in. Next to that was another, called *Ralighe*, a lying down, which was large but rather less than the first. Next to that were *Beran*, a crevice, and *Shimidaran*, mallet, lesser than Ralighe, and they would accommodate 12 men each to sleep in. Next to that was *Leaba nan Con*, or the dogs' bed, and next to that was *Leaba an Tealich*, or the Fireside bed. There was an entrance (passage) in the wall round about, by which they might go from one croop to another without coming into the central chamber. The house was not to be noticed outside, except a small hole in the top of it, to allow the smoke to get out and to let in some light. There was a doorway on one side (where they had to bend to get in and out) facing the sea, and a large hill of ashes a little way from the door, which would not allow the wind to come in. *Bar Righ*, top of the shieling, was the name of the door.' The roof fell in around 1840 and much of the stone must have been used in building the three bothies.

Macaulay has a similar description but reckoned that the four beds could take four men each!

Carry on northwards to the arête at the foot of Clagan na Rùsgachan.

CLAGAN NA RÙSGACHAN, SKULL ROCK OF THE FLEECES

It is an impressive rock tower 240m (789 ft) supporting three pinnacles. It gives the appearance of a skull from certain angles; below the main tower was a hollow used by

Bothy on Boreray, Clagan na Rùsgachan behind.

These are remains of one of the three bothies on Boreray used by the St Kilda men when they stayed for 1-2 weeks to attend their sheep and kill gannets. They were also used by the women when they came to catch puffins.

the St Kildans to shear their sheep – hence, Skull Rock of the Fleeces. The highest concentration of nesting gannets is to be found here – some 2,000 pairs on this buttress and on the extensive ledges of *Clesgor*, Cliff-gash, which is about 76m (250ft) above the sea, facing north-west. By St Kildan standards it was one of the more accessible nesting sites and the gannet-hunters' ledges are well defined. Peter Moore accompanied Stuart Murray, 'along a gannet-hunters' route into an area where the sheep cannot reach. It was a remarkable experience, we followed the "obvious" route – not doing anything smart or looking for problems and along the way, one could find evidence that feet had passed that way in antiquity; rocks wedged into cracks to form steps, jammed across faults as well as small bridges, presumably to aid the passage of laden gannet-hunters and, of course, the large two part bridge that Stuart discovered in the 1970s, which is the only way across one very large rock fault in the whole of its 700 foot length.'

Between the Cleit Village and this rock it is estimated that 41,000 pairs of puffins nest – the largest colony on Boreray.

Continue along the cliff edge track north-east of Clagan na Rùsgachan on rising ground.

CLAIS NA RÙNAICH, THE HOLLOW OR FURROW OF THE BELOVED

Look down into Clais na Rùnaich where the steep rift falls headlong into the sea and the grassy areas support another large puffin colony, beyond, Stac Lee is seen far below.

Carry on up the slope following the cliff edge, make a detour out to the west along the ridge for close up views of gannet ledges, then on to Na Roàchan.

NA ROÀCHAN

Na Roàchan (possibly the Wrinkled or Corrugated Rocks, alternatively, the Preferred Ones or something to do with The Throats – the choice is yours!) is a great rock tower of

The grass clad slopes of Sunadal on Boreray are riddled with the nest burrows for 17,000 pairs of puffins. The gannet cliffs lie beyond with ledges for guillemots and kittiwakes below.

382m (1,252 ft). With its great buttresses and rock walls, looking along to the north, the gannet cliffs are at their most magnificent, plunging down to the sea 366m (1,200 ft) below.

From Na Roàchan strike across to Mullach an Eilean.

MULLACH AN EILEAN, ISLAND SUMMIT (384m, 1,259ft)

Strike up to Mullach an Eilean with its strange undulating ridge falling away vertically on the left, and on the right the hair-raising grassy slope of Sunadal sweeps down to the sea to the east.

Peter Moore admirably describes the scene along the ridge: 'Mullach an Eilean extends north in a series of spectacular undulations of its knife-edge, until it plunges into a gully rising from *Geò na Tarnanach*, Thunder Cave. This forms a natural barrier to anything other than "technical" exploration. I have been on Boreray only once in the company of anyone competent enough to support or undertake exploration of that nature and on that occasion we explored other areas of the island. As a result, I have not crossed the Tarnanach Gully on either the east or the west and have not reached An t-Sail on foot. The mixture of ledges, gannets, puffins and sheep on Boreray, together with the excellent weather that I have usually experienced, is an intoxicating concoction. The view across the archipelago from the Tigh Stallar area is undoubtedly my favourite in the whole group.'

The highest of the twin towers on *An t-Sail*, the Heel, stands at 240m (788ft).

An t-Sail, Boreray with Stac an Armin behind. A steep gully nearly separates the vertical rocks of An t-Sail (260m, 788ft) from the summit ridge of Boreray, Thunder Cave is at the foot. Large numbers of gannets nest on the ledges.

SCOTTISH BLACKFACE SHEEP

This type of sheep was brought over from Lewis but was not introduced into St Kilda until 1872. Those on Boreray may be encountered practically anywhere on the island but they are extremely wild and soon disappear out of sight. With thicker and larger fleeces than the Soay Sheep (not found here) they are better able to resist the wind and suffer less from heat loss. They demonstrate their hardiness by having survived on this outpost untended since the evacuation. The last count in 1987 was 369. Their success is partly due to the luxuriant growth of grass for six months of the year, the best being found in Sunadal where the remains of fish brought in and the droppings of the birds add valuable nutrients. At the evacuation of St Kilda in 1930 it was not possible to gather these sheep and take them off the island.

SEABIRD NUMBERS

At the last count in 1987, on Boreray alone there were storm and Leach's petrels present, small numbers of nesting shags (2), gulls in territories, lesser black-backed (12), greater black-backed (15), herring (38), kittiwake (2,923), great skuas (2). Individual guillemots (3,679), razorbills (252), black guillemots (5). Puffins 63,000 occupied burrows, fulmars 6,802 sites and gannets 24,676 nests.

Return to the boat by the same route. If time permits make a detour to Mullach an Tuamail.

Boreray - west face. An amazing wall of near vertical rock surmounted by towers and turrets, gouged out gullies and eroded sea caves. Home to thousands of nesting gannets and puffins, also kittiwakes, guillemots and razorbills. Left to right: An t-Sail, Geò na Tarnanach, Mullach an Eilein (summit), Na Roàchan, Clais na Rùnaich, Clagan na Rùsgachan and Clesgor.

Stac Lee

THE BLUE STAC, MAJESTIC ROCK (172m, 564ft)
Stac Lee rises vertically 220m (720ft) from the sea bed, 172m (564ft) above the surface of the sea. From every angle it is spectacular: Sir Julian Huxley assessed it as 'the most majestic sea rock in existence'. From a distance it lives up to its name, 'The Blue Stac' – the blue hue derived from the thousands of gannets. At close quarters it has a sparkling white roof of nesting gannets. From the south it appears as a massive flat unclimbable wall with a few sloping white ledges; from the west its sides are vertical with the summit ridge sliced off at a 45 degree angle. The most impressive view is from the south-east where it rises out of the water like a huge fang. Wilson (1842) describes it well: 'The whole presenting the appearance of some huge marine monster, of which the upper jaw was raised aloft and the under stretched out horizontally, prepared to snap up a ship or two, or a thousand solan geese in one fell swoop.' From the north-east it is complete with the monster's eye and white gannet teeth! Kearton regarded this pillar of rock as, 'one of the wonders of the world.'

Below the surface it is just as impressive. Gordon Ridley describes many dives in his book, including the east corner of Stac Lee, 'This dive follows probably the grandest rock wall in British waters...the wall is a gentle overhang from the surface to the seafloor 50m below. Its surface is completely filmed with a riot of browns and yellows, oranges and reds, and blues and greens. Exhaled air slowly trickles to the surface glistening through this biological barrier. Even in a long diving career this is a dive to cherish.' He also describes diving at Geò Lee, where the cliff and the seabed meet there is a fault line which has formed a cleft with a series of entrances, gullies, tunnels and caverns. At the back of the cleft is a continuous tunnel

Stac Lee, the 'blue stac'. Tooth-like from some angles, wall-like from others, it is 172 metres high and is regarded by many as one of the wonders of the world.

137

which narrows before widening and rounding a corner into an unexplored chamber.

No less remarkable is the bothy at a height of 120m, built on a ledge below an overhang. It was used by the gannet-hunters in August and September when they took the gugas, and possibly in March when they went for the adults. Peter Moore surveyed it in detail: 'The siting of the bothy is probably linked both to the ready availability of building material, which would have been gathered from the shattered summit slopes, and to its position affording ready access to the summit colony. There is an early account of water being available. The overhang provided a dry shelter which needed only to be enclosed. This was partially accomplished by the placing of two large boulders each 0.9m long and about 0.56m high, which dominate the interior of the wall. Around and on top of these, smaller, angular rocks are piled in the form of cladding in an arc approximately 4m high and set slightly downhill at the centre; the overhanging rock forms an angled lintel and a threshold slab has been laid. Inside, the floor is level and the roof, which reaches a maximum height of 1.65m, slopes towards the back. Left of the doorway is a raised stone platform, some 0.3m above the floor, which may have been used to sleep on, though the proximity of an aperture in the roof suggests a use as a base for a fire. However, there is no evidence of blackened stone or ash, but if a stay of several days were envisaged then fuel, possibly cut turves, may well have been brought and gannet nesting material also used. Another possible reason for this aperture is that there was no suitably sized building material available to complete the corbelled roof.'

Stac Lee from the southeast. Stac Lee rears up like a sea monster with jaws gaping ready to swallow in one mouthful several boats or a thousand gannets.

NESTING SEABIRDS

At the last estimate the stac was home to 13,521 pairs of gannets, 39 pairs of fulmars, 245 pairs of kittiwakes, 490 individual guillemots and 15 razorbills – no puffins. In the past there were many more guillemots and razorbills on the ledges but these have been ousted by the gannets. The St Kildans never removed eggs from Stac Lee as they wanted

to reap the best harvest of gannets, and later in the season they would take 5-7,000 gugas from this stac alone each year for food.

LANDING ON THE STAC

Landing caused few problems for the St Kildans. They had a metal peg in the rock around which they threw a rope, a second rope was attached to the first climber; the swell might be 3-6m (10-20ft), as the boat arose he would step off onto a narrow ledge. Through long experience, agility and bare feet, the slippery seaweed, swell and breaking waves seemed to cause no extra difficulties for St Kildans. Others have found it more exacting. Heathcote, who climbed the stac with his sister in 1898 wrote, 'We both failed to get any foothold, and were hauled up after the fashion of a sack of potatoes.'

Stac Lee from the west.
Stac Lee is home to over 13,500 pairs of nesting gannets of which 5,000 pairs are on the sloping roof of the rock. St Kildans visited this stac at night in March to collect adult gannets.

OLIVER PIKE'S VISIT IN 1910

The mind boggles at the thought of Oliver Pike landing in 1910 with his huge ciné camera: 'The model made by Pathé – with two large film boxes on the top which held 400ft of film. The tripod was an equally massive affair. However, with my two friends from the mainland and three natives, we were able to get all the apparatus about.' He recalled, 'No sooner had we left the jetty than I heard the most excited shout from my crew of six. The sea was rushing through a small hole in the boat, but a cork, that was no doubt kept handy for such a mishap, was quickly hammered into the leak, and we proceeded. Directly we left the bay and rounded the cliffs leading to the open sea, we met the wind, and had to row hard for three solid hours against wind and tide. One of my oarsmen happened to be 80 just that day but he pulled the whole distance without once stopping, although his younger companions twice changed oars... As I looked above to the towering rocks, I had to admit that it was quite impossible for any human being to scale the precipitous sides, and I said as much to the only native who understood English. But he assured me that I should get to the top...'

'After a strenuous climb we were half way up. Several times we had to take the cameras from our backs; then one climber going upwards pulled them up after him. In other difficult places we had to crawl along narrow ledges, clinging on tightly to crevices with our hands, while beneath was a sheer drop of three hundred feet… At last we reached the summit…The top of this famous rock has been the home of the gannets for probably thousands of years past… When that great flock of birds saw the five strangers in their home they panicked. They tried to rise but just tumbled back and struggling on, tumbling over each other in their excitement. Five thousand great white birds… All around the air was white with passing wings, like giant snowflakes falling on a living snowfield of birds… After spending a couple of hours in that weird scene, we prepared to descend. I have always hated going down a cliff… When I saw the leading climber creep round that corner with practically nothing between him and the sea, I wondered if I should succeed in getting down. The footholds for our feet were exceedingly small, some only one inch in width, and there seemed to be hardly a niche in which to place our fingers. Taking the equipment from my back, and even any projecting things from my pockets I essayed to follow… I was expecting the cameras to be damaged or dropped, but they survived this rough usage, merely bearing to this day large dents and scratches as monograms inscribed by the rocks of St Kilda. We at last reached our boat. I felt pleased with my day's work, and happier still after returning home and seeing the films projected. They proved to be a great success in those early days of ciné pictures, shown in almost every town where there were cinemas, all over the Continent, America and the Colonies' (Pike, 1946).

A RECENT CLIMB – 1990
On 21 May Jon Warren, Andrew Elwell, an experienced climber, and Steve Holloway, the Warden, climbed the stac and collected gannet eggs for analysis. Some extracts of Jon's account follow: 'Arriving at the great rock, the

Stac Lee was vital to the St Kildans for the guga (young gannet) harvest. Centuries ago they built a bothy high up under an overhanging rock for shelter, in case the weather changed and the catch was lost. Stac Lee also plunges deep under the water, with its many fault lines, caves and a wealth of marine life, allowing divers a magnificent experience.

walls were indeed vertical with hanging forests of oarweed (kelp) clinging horizontally for three metres above my head. Amazingly, there was a convenient ledge just above the surface of the water, which made jumping onto the rock easier. The kelp gave way to a layer of barnacles and dark green algae, which thankfully was tinder dry. In 6m (20ft) we were on a good ledge... Streaked white with chemical deposits leached from the rock, the vertical precipice above looked menacing. Six metres above us a wide friendly ledge ran diagonally to the left. To reach this we ascended a near vertical rock wall. Had the rock been wet, this stretch would have been treacherous. At about 37m (120 ft) the ledge zig zagged to the right – we scaled 4m of exposed rock. In another 27m our pathway came to an abrupt end. We had reached the pitch!'

The Pitch – 'The next part of the ascent involved climbing an 11m vertical wall of exposed rock... The gabbro surface was so badly weathered and smoothed that

there was virtually nowhere to place gear with any
effectiveness in the event of a fall... We reached the top of
the famous Pitch and were now at about 60m (200ft). It
had taken 20 adrenalin pumping minutes of total
concentration... The sun shone brightly onto the glassy
sea, and the air was completely still apart from the whistle
of gannets' wings as they flew past. We were on a 6ft ledge
and we knew that round the corner the gannets would
increase dramatically. After passing the corner, the ledge
led upwards and westwards across the face of the stac, at an
angle of about 35 degrees. Ahead, we were confronted by a
wall of gannets that seemed to occupy every space available
to them...we approached a massive overhang. Our route
took us underneath this huge projection of rock. Hugging
the wall of the overhang on a 3ft wide ledge we came
across five guillemots incubating eggs.'

The Bothy – 'Stepping over countless gannet nests we
neared the end of the overhang. Before us we could see a
wide platform...that led to the summit slopes. At the
beginning of the platform, tucked into the extreme left-
hand edge of the overhang, we found the bothy. It was
built by the St Kildans to use as a shelter for an advance
party prior to the gannet harvest in case rough weather
prevented them landing and therefore losing their whole
catch... Unfortunately we could not venture inside as two
fulmars were each incubating eggs.'

The Summit – 'On reaching the top of the bothy platform,
the sight before us defied description. Thousands upon
thousands of gannets sat tightly on their weed and flotsam
built nests, completely swamping the huge summit slopes in
a white blanket of birds. To reach the summit we would
need to climb another 30m (100ft) through massed gannet
ranks. Understandably we were reluctant to disturb the
gannets. To minimise this we decided to walk up the left-
hand ridge of the stac. The bevelled slope led up at an
angle of about 45 degrees. As we ascended towards the
summit, the broken ground underfoot surprised me, with

loose shattered rock of varying sizes littering the slope…
Close to the summit a blizzard of gannets took to the air
causing a minor dust-storm which actually blurred our
vision. It was truly an amazing experience… The views
from the summit were of unbelievable dimensions!'

ST KILDANS CLIMBED AT NIGHT

In his 1793 book Buchanan gives this account of the men
working along a ledge at night in April, roped to each
other in case of a fall, first going to take the sentinel
gannet: 'The fowler, with a white towel about his breast,
calmly slides over the face of the rocks till he has a full
view of the sentinel. Then he gently moves along on his
hands and feet, creeping very silently to the spot where the
sentinel stands on guard. If he cries "bir, bir" the sign of
alarm, he stands back: but if he cries, "grog, grog", that of
confidence, he advances without fear of giving an alarm
because the goose takes the fowler for one of the straggling
geese coming into the camp, and suffers him to advance.
Then the fowler very gently tickles one of his legs which
he lifts and places on the palm of his hand; he then as
gently tickles the other, which in like manner is lifted and
placed on his hand. He then no less artfully than insensibly
moves the sentinel near the first sleeping goose, which he
pushes with his fingers; on which he awakes, and finding
the sentinel standing above him, he immediately falls a
fighting him for his supposed insolence. This alarms the
whole camp, and instead of flying off they begin to fight
through the whole company; while in the meantime the
common enemy, unsuspected, begins in good earnest to
twist their necks, and never gives up till the whole are left
dead on the spot…a man told me that he was one of four
men that catched four itts or pens, being 300 each, in the
whole 1,200 geese in one night.

When they came later in the year for the gugas,
having killed them, they took them to the Casting Point
where they threw them into the water to be collected up by
the men in the boat…until they cried "Enough!" '

Stac Lee from the 'cleit village' on Boreray.
One of the most
impressive views of Stac
Lee, which rises like a
fang from the sea, is from
the cleit village on
Boreray.

144

Stac an Armin

THE WARRIOR'S STAC (196m, 644ft)

Stac an Armin was said to commemorate a knight of Lochlann. They had a saying in Gaelic, 'There could be no cause for fear on Hirta as they had the Boar (*An Torc*) to the west and the Knight to the east.'

It is the highest sea-stac in Britain and rises from the sea as a massive rock wedge with an overhang towards Hirta. Its southern sloping side is made up of a series of giant rock steps with boulder screes between. From the north, in a small boat, there is a moment when three spiky peaks appear; another when the sheer vertical face plunges into the sea with waves smashing against the base and exploding inside a huge overhang where the watery impact has already gouged out great chunks of volcanic rock.

With their clinker-built boats, St Kildans required a vertical rock face with convenient ledges. As the boat rose in the swell they could get a toe hold on the ledge and a few finger grips above – stockinged feet gave the best purchase. Here they found such a place at the south east corner, just north of *Am Biran*, 'sharp-pointed one', a great sharp sloping wedge. This landing can only be accomplished if the wind is in the north-west. The south-west corner with its fractured rocks, *Rubha Bhriste*, 'broken rounded headland', was not suitable for them to land. Today there must always be a scientific purpose for landing.

ASCENT AND THE BIRDS

Having landed, the ascent is reasonably easy compared with climbing Stac Lee. Keep to the right over some steep rocks up to the bothy and the cleitean. From here it is possible to pick a way between the three main gannet colonies so that there is minimum disturbance. Gannets nest all round and on top of the massive blocks of gabbro at

Stac an Armin, the highest sea-stac in Britain at 196 metres, has many vertical faces above water and a knife-edge ridge below. It was the enforced winter home for three men and eight boys from August 1727 until May of the following year. They lived in a bothy and inevitably suffered much from cold and hunger. The stac is home for nearly 12,000 pairs of nesting gannets, guillemots, kittiwakes, fulmars and usually two or three pairs of St Kilda wrens.

145

the summit, with razorbills and guillemots below the boulders. There are splendid rocky slopes and broad ledges for the 11,853 pairs of nesting gannets, fewer than on Stac Lee. But on this stac there are larger numbers of fulmars; 2,387 occupied sites; 1,436 guillemots; 237 razorbills; also 100 occupied burrows of puffins and 326 nest sites of kittiwakes. Wrens and rock pipits also nest among the boulders. A great auk was killed here in 1840.

CLEITEAN AND BOTHY

Sheep were put on here in winter to make use of the sparse vegetation. Mary Harman recently counted as many as 78 cleitean, some being just vestiges of a cleit with only a few stones on a curve remaining, others with their lintels intact. They were spread over the middle slope of the stac up to about 150m (500ft), level with the highest of the colonies of gannets. In the 1700s, they held surplus gugas which had been killed but not salted. During the winter these dried out to be shipped back to Hirta the next year.

One small bothy, larger than a cleit and with two windows, sits on a ledge about 125m above the sea. Used regularly during the gannet harvest, it was 'home' for a landing party of three men and eight boys in August 1727. On the rock to collect young gannets and feathers, they expected to stay for a week or two. However, an outbreak of smallpox on Hirta was so severe that a crew could not be mustered to rescue them. It caused 94 deaths, leaving only four adults and 26 children from 21 families. The group on the stac were marooned until the middle of May the next year when the factor came and found them all well.

THE END OF FEARCHAR MÓR

The sheep stealing brothers from Lewis, having pillaged animals on the Flannan islands, came to St Kilda adding murder to their crimes. Eventually exposed and captured, it was here that the infamous Fearchar Mór chose to fling himself into the turbulent waters rather than end his days on this inhospitable rock! Dugan died in isolation on Soay.

A RECENT VISIT

In May 1994 Jim Vaughan, the Warden, who with Jon Warren and Andy Elwell went on the stac to collect gannet eggs reported, 'We landed at Rubha Briste. The ascent began with a traverse around the base slabs passing close under a sizeable guillemot colony to a point just opposite An t-Sail... A third of the way up we located the bothy which was constructed just below the base of a cliff. Although roofless, the wall and lintel were intact and in a very good state of repair. The structure was tenanted by several nesting fulmars...south from here we ascended another steep mud bank, scrambling over a short rock wall to be met by the first main gannet colony,... Hirta came back into view... On reaching the small summit gannet colony, which we now passed through, we were surprised how little disturbance we had caused on our way to the top... The view of Boreray from the summit, without doubt, is the finest we had experienced.'

One of the finest views in the archipelago reveals itself as the boat passes between the east side of Boreray and Stac an Armin, looking to the main island group. At first Am Plastair is seen, then quickly the great bulk of Soay, the stacs in Soay Sound and the Cambir. Stac Lee then interposes itself partly obscuring Conachair, next Oiseval and lastly Dùn. In the foreground the rocks off Boreray complete the indescribably majestic scene.

Stac Lee, Stac an Armin and Boreray. Having left Village Bay to visit Boreray and the Stacs, this view is majestic and awe-inspiring. Home to over 50,000 pairs of nesting gannets, these rocks form the far side of the rim of the ancient volcano.

1830-44 Rev. Neil MacKenzie became the first resident minister for over 100 years. He was appointed in 1829 and was introduced to the St Kildans on 4 July 1830 by Dr John MacDonald. He was the mastermind behind the 'new village' of the 1830s.

1830 During the first half of the year Christ Church was erected on its present site at the cost of £600 and the manse was completed.

1831 The naturalist G .C. Atkinson visited.

1834 Sir Thomas Dyke Acland visited in his yacht *Lady of St Kilda*. He left 20 guineas with the minister for the first person to demolish and rebuild his own house, stimulating the new village.

1834-38 The improved 'thatched houses', or '1834 Houses' were built on their present site. The Head Dyke was also erected .

1835 A Prussian vessel foundered off St Kilda. The crew of 11 made it safely to shore.

1838 The *Vulcan* called at St Kilda, the first tourist vessel to do so, with a brass band, and Lachlan MacLean, writer, together with two ecclesiastical men, Dr Dickson and Dr MacLeod. For some time Village Bay was called 'Dickson's Bay' and Glen Bay, 'MacLeod's'.

1839 The *Charlotte* of Hull was wrecked on Rockall. Eighteen of the crew landed on Hirta and stayed for 11 days.

1840 John MacGillivray, naturalist, visited.

1841 James Wilson FRSE MWS, author and traveller, visited St Kilda and made the first census of the inhabitants.

1846 St Kildans declared their adherence to the Free Church in the presence of a Deputy visiting the island.

1847 A visit is made by Sir W. M. E. Milner, a zoologist, who landed on Boreray.

1851 A teacher was sent out by the Free Church Ladies Association.

1852 The *Priscilla* left for Melbourne, Australia with 36 St Kildans on board: 20 died of fever on the way.

1853 Dr John MacKenzie visited on board *S/V Jessie*.

1856-63 Duncan Kennedy, Catechist and Registrar, was sent by the Free Church.

1858 T. S. Muir, a writer concerned with ecclesiological matters visited.

1858 A visit was made by Sharbau from 8-9 July. He mapped out the Village and contents of the cleitean.

1860 John E. Morgan arrived to investigate the 'boat cold' along with Capt. Thomas R. N., folklore specialist, and the Duke of Athole on *HMS Porcupine*.

1860 3 October. A terrific storm carried off several roofs and the *Porcupine* with Capt. Otter was nearly lost.

1860 Sharbau published his Village map.

1861 Alex Grigor, Examiner of Registers, visited on *Porcupine*, the Admiralty Survey Ship.

1861-2 Sixteen new cottages were built.

1863 April. A boating tragedy struck; seven men and one woman, Betty Scott, were lost from the *Dargavel* en route to Harris.

1864 7 April. *Janet Cowan* went aground on the rocks in dense fog. She was on the way from Calcutta to Dundee with a cargo of jute. The captain and crew were saved and the bell was used by the Church.

1865 October. The Rev. John MacKay became Minister of the Free Church on St Kilda for 24 years.

1868 The naturalist H. J. Elwes visited.

1869 31 May. Euphemia MacCrimmon, the last of the *senachie*, or verbal historians, died aged 88.

1871 St Kilda was sold back to Norman, 22nd Chief of MacLeod. The islands remained in the family until 1934.

1871 The factor visited three times in the 80 ton sailing schooner, the *Robert Hadden*.

1871 Alex Grigor, Examiner of Registers, visited on *HMS Jackall*.

1873 Dr R. Angus Smith visited on the *Nyanza*.

1874 Sir William and Lady Baillie of Polkemmet visited.

1875 John Sands, writer, visited. He was marooned from 1876-7, on his second visit and finally rescued by *HMS Jackall*.

1877 17 January. The captain and eight of the crew of *Peti Dabrovacki* landed after being shipwrecked off St Kilda. They stayed five weeks.

1877 30 January. The first 'mail boat' was launched by Sands and a message reached the Austrian Embassy.

1877 Lord and Lady MacDonald visited in the yacht *Lady of the Isles*, along with Miss MacLeod of MacLeod, the daughter of the proprietor, who stayed in

1877   the Factor's House.
2 July. *Dunara Castle* reached St Kilda on the first Western Isles Cruise and was to visit regularly until the outbreak of World War Two in 1939. In the party of about 40 was George Seton, Advocate and author – they landed for four hours.

1878   SS *Mastiff* visited on her way to Iceland with Anthony Trollope on board.

1882   The crops failed. In April men went to Skye in a small fishing boat to obtain food.

1883   June. A Commission of Inquiry, the Napier Commission, was held on Hirta.

1883   R. M. Barrington visited. A botanist, he explored every corner of the islands, climbing Stac Biorach.

1884   Charles Dixon visited and collected mice from which H. Seebohm named the new sub-species of field mouse.

1884   Mr Campbell arrived, the first school-master sponsored by the Ladies Society of the Free Church. A room in the Factor's House was made available to him as a schoolroom.

1884-6   Ann McKinlay was the resident nurse.

1885   A storm ruined the crops. Alex Ferguson launched a mail boat which resulted in supplies being sent.

1885-6   Two visits were made by Robert Connell, author and journalist with the *Glasgow Herald*.

1885-6   Hugh MacCullum was schoolmaster.

1886-7   The schoolmaster, George Murray, kept a diary. The school was held in the Kirk.

1887   Alfred Newton visited with E. and J. Wolley and Henry Evans.

1888-9   Mr McRee was schoolmaster.

1888   Henry Evans from Jura, who had made nine previous visits, visited again.

1889   Mr John Ross, the schoolmaster, wrote fascinating account of his stay.

1889-1903   Rev. Angus Fiddes, was the last of the ordained Free Church Ministers on the island. He went to Glasgow to find a cure for infantile tetanus.

1892   Alex Ferguson emigrated to Glasgow and became a successful cloth merchant.

1894   Visits were made by Ellis Malcolm who was collecting for H. A. MacPherson, and J. S. Elliot. Steele Elliot was the first person to recognise two species of mice on St Kilda, and thought the Wren were reduced to 15 pairs.

1895   Sir Archibald Geikie, geologist, J. Wolly and H. Evans visited. They returned the following year.

1896   Richard and Cherry Kearton, photographers and naturalists visited.

1898   Masons and carpenters from Dunvegan began to build the new schoolroom.

1898   The SS *Hebrides* called; she was to call several times each summer.

1898   Norman Heathcote, naturalist and author, visited with his sister. Both climbed Stac Lee and were present at the laying of the foundation stone of the school. They paid a second visit in 1899.

1899   Henry Evans of Jura visited for the twelfth time.

1900   The Church was now supported by the United Free Church of Scotland.

1900-1   James MacKenzie was schoolmaster.

1900   July. The St Kilda Post Office became fully operational for the first time in the lower floor of the Factor's House with the Rev. Angus Fiddes as sub-postmaster.

1902   July-August. Mary Mackenzie from the Royal Academy in Inverness was teacher.

1902   Dr Wigglesworth, ornithologist and writer, visited and climbed Boreray and some of the stacs.

1903   Lachlan MacLean was missionary.

1903   July-August. Edith Finlay from Central School in Inverness was schoolteacher.

1903-6   John Fraser was missionary.

1903-4   Mr MacDonald was schoolmaster.

1903   J. A. Harvey-Brown, naturalist and author, visited.

1904   July-August. Kathleen Kennedy from the High School in Inverness was teacher.

1904   The bill introduced to parliament by Sir Herbert Maxwell was passed and The Wild Birds Protection (St Kilda) Act became law.

1904-5   Mr R. MacDonald was the schoolmaster.

1905   The naturalist J. Waterston visited.

1905   July-August. Miss W. Gollan was schoolteacher.

1906-9   Peter MacLachlan was on St Kilda as the missionary, with his wife Alice who was the schoolteacher. Their daughter Susan was born on St Kilda in 1909.

1906   Neil Ferguson senior became sub-postmaster until the evacuation.

1907   Bentley Beetham, bird photographer, and Harry Brazenor, a collector, visited.

1908	Oliver Pike, an early ciné-photographer of birds, and Bentley Beetham visited.
1909	22 March. A dreadful boating tragedy struck; Donald MacDonald, Norman and John MacQueen were drowned.
1909-12	Miss Annie MacLean from Glasgow was schoolteacher.
1910	Oliver Pike, the Duchess of Bedford and W. Eagle Clarke all visited.
1910-11	Eagle Clarke prepared 60 skins of Field and 40 of House Mice.
1911	J. H. Gurney, author of *The Gannet* visited.
1912	HMS *Achilles* called with supplies after a trawler had found the people starving.
1912-4	Mr MacArthur was missionary.
1913	The Post Office was now situated in the corrugated iron hut between Cottages No. 4 and No. 5.
1913	29 July. A wireless station was installed in the Factor's House. Messages were sent to the King, and to the *Daily Mirror* which had led the campaign for the transmitter.
1914-19	Alex MacKinnon was missionary with his wife who was a schoolteacher.
1914	E. W. Wade and the Duchess of Bedford made visits.
1915	12 January. A signal station was set up near the store-house, and manned by naval ratings based on Aultbea, later from Stornoway.
1918	15 May. Hirta was shelled by a German submarine.
1919	The naval garrison was evacuated and the wireless station closed down.
1919-26	Donald Cameron was missionary, with his wife Mary and two daughters, Mary and Christina.
1924	William MacDonald of Cottage No. 3 was the first to leave with his whole family.
1925	Donald John Gillies left for Glasgow, then Toronto. He became a Presbyterian minister.
1926	Four St Kildan men died of influenza.
1926	Nurse Littlejohn was working there.
1926-9	John MacLeod was missionary and schoolteacher, with his wife and two boys, Alexander and Kenneth.
1927	Nurse Flett was in residence on Hirta.
1927	Seton Gordon, naturalist and author visited.
1927	The islands were surveyed by John Mathieson, assisted by A. M. Cockburn.
1928	A. M. Cockburn continued and

	completed his geological survey work of St Kilda.
1928	Nurse Williamina Barclay arrived on the island and stayed until the evacuation.
1929-30	Dugald Munro was missionary and teacher, with his wife Ann.
1929	The bird photographer F. A. Lowe visited.
1930	15 February. The fishery cruiser *Norna* called to take off Mary Gillies with appendicitis.
1930	August. The evacuation of St Kilda. On Thursday 28 August *Dunara Castle* was loaded with 573 sheep, 13 cattle and mail. It left at 12 noon for Oban. On Friday 29 HMS *Harebell* took the remainder of furniture and effects with the islanders to Lochaline and Oban. The events were recorded by Alasdair Alpin MacGregor, a *Times* correspondent and author. The evacuation was filmed by John Ritchie.
1931	The Oxford and Cambridge University Expedition produced the *St Kilda Papers*.
1931	5 September. Sir Reginald MacLeod sold the islands to the 5th Marquis of Bute.
1932	The Marquis of Bute transferred 107 Soay Sheep from Soay to Hirta.
1939	17 August. *Dunara Castle* left Glasgow on her last scheduled sailing to St Kilda.
1948	*Dunara Castle*, after 73 years serving the Western Isles, went to the breakers yard.
1956	St Kilda was bequeathed to the National Trust for Scotland by the Marquis of Bute, on his death on 14 August
1957	St Kilda was accepted by the National Trust for Scotland. An Ordnance Survey Team worked on the official map of St Kilda. The Air Ministry sent an RAF Task Force, 'Hard Rock', consisting of 300 officers and men to begin work on the road, camp and tracking station.
1957	J. Morton Boyd was appointed as scientist in charge of the St Kilda National Nature Reserve.
1958	The Nature Conservancy Council took over the management of St Kilda as a National Nature Reserve. The first of the St Kilda Working Parties arranged by the NTS Formation of the St Kilda Club.
1958	A joint schools expedition was led by Alex Warwick. In August, Royal Artillery took over from the RAF. The road to Mullach Mór was completed by

	November. The Decca radar was installed.
1959	A catching, tagging and measuring programme of Soay Sheep started.
1959	Hammond Innes visited St Kilda on an LCT (Landing Craft, Tank) and was inspired to write *Island Fury*.
1959	8 November. Thirteen trawlers, 10 Spanish, sheltered from a gale in Village Bay.
1960	June. *The Avocet*, a 50 ton yawl, chartered by the NTS, was wrecked on the rocks of Village Bay. The main mast was salvaged and erected as a flagpole for the detachment.
1962	The officers' mess was completed and the Factor's House was handed back to the NTS.
1963	Summer. A detachment of 29 soldiers and 120 civilians undertook major work on the camp and the Royal Engineers deepened the jetty.
1964	Research on the Field Mouse began. P. A. Jewell trapped 36 on Hirta and in 1967 R. J. Berry trapped 42.
1966	A hydrographic team from the Royal Navy started surveying the sea around St Kilda.
1968	Gavin Ferguson returns for the first time since the evacuation.
1969	The first survey of puffins began. It was carried on by M. P. Harris and S. Murray for the entire breeding seasons of 1974-6.
1969	Work on a new army camp and an extension to the jetty were almost complete.
1971	The Royal Family visited on the Royal Yacht, and were filmed by John Wilkie.
1971	An ITV production team visit to make the documentary *A Far Better Place*.
1974	The fishing boat *Marian* was wrecked in the Village Bay.
1976	The first weather reports, requested by the Meteorological Office, were sent to Benbecula.
1977	A bonfire was lit on Conachair to commemorate the Silver Jubilee.
1977	Mary Harman began her field surveys and research into cleitean and other buildings.
1979	A plaque was placed in the Kirk to commemorate the crews of the aircraft which crashed on St Kilda during World War Two.
1980	27 August. A service of Rededication of the Kirk was held on the 50th Anniversary of the Evacuation.
1981	A charter boat, *Golden Chance*, wrecked in Village Bay.
1981	December. *Maersk Angus*, an oil tanker, drifted out of control off Hirta.
1982-3	House No. 3 was repaired and turned into the museum.
1984-7	The Feather Store was repaired and reroofed.
1985	New archaeological studies and studies on the Soay sheep were begun.
1987	Jerold James Gordon won an International Award for his 'St Kilda Requiem'.
1987	10 August. In a ceremony in the Kirk, St Kilda was designated a World Heritage Site, the first in Scotland.
1987	Gordon Gibb windsurfed to St Kilda, travelling 65 miles in 10hrs 50min.
1988	Exciting archaeological finds were discovered by House No. 8. The conservancy work on sheep and seabird numbers continued.
1989	January. A mailboat launched in August 1988 was picked up on the Lofoten Islands in Norway.
1989	June. Canoeist David Hayter made the first solo trip to St Kilda; it was a near disaster.
1989	Archaeologists discovered the corn drying kiln behind the Factor's House.
1990	During two weeks of the summer, David Stansfield contacted 600 Radio Amateurs from St Kilda.
1990	August. The 60th Anniversary of the Evacuation.
1991	The army demolished their old buildings on Mullach Mór.
1991	Robert Atkinson photographs were donated to the NTS.
1991	Donald Thompson became the first to canoe to St Kilda and back!
1992	Paul Reisch sailed to St Kilda in a 16ft Wayfarer dinghy, *Windy Wells*.
1993	Archaeological work began on the St. Brendan's site. The army detachment was reduced to only eight men.
1995	4 March. The trawler *Aeolus* went aground on the rocks near Boreray. One man died, four were rescued.

Plant Checklist

Angelica, Wild - *Angelica sylvestris*
Asphodel, Bog - *Narthecium ossifragum*

Bedstraw, Heath - *Galium saxatile*
Bitter-cress, Wavy - *Cardamine flexuosa*
Blaeberry - *Vaccinium myrtillus*
Blinks - *Montia fonatana*
Bugle - *Ajuga reptans*
Buttercup, Meadow - *Ranunculus acris*
Butterwort, Common - *Pinguicula vulgaris*

Celandine, Lesser - *Ranunculus ficaria*
Chickweed, Common - *Stellaria media*
Clover, White - *Trifolium repens*
Clubmoss, Fir - *Huperzia selago*
   Lesser - *Selaginella selaginoides*

Cotton Grass - *Eriophorum angustifolium*
Cowberry - *Vaccinium vitis-idaea*
Crowberry - *Empetrum nigrum*

Daisy - *Bellis perennis*
Dandelion - *Taraxacum sp.*
Deergrass - *Scirpus cespitosus*
Dock, Broad-leaved - *Rumex obtusifolius*
   Clustered - *Rumex conglomeratus*
   Curled - *Rumex crispus*

Eyebright - *Euphrasia sp.*

Ferns, Adder's Tongue - *Ophioglossum vulgatum*
   Brittle Bladder-Fern - *Cysteropteris fragilis*
   Black Spleenwort - *Asplenium adiantum-nigrum*
   Bracken - *Pteridium aquilinum*
   Broad Buckler-Fern - *Dryopteris dilatata*
   Hard - *Blenchnum spicant*
   Lady-Fern - *Athyrium filix-femina*
   Moonwort - *Botrychium lunaria*
   Polypody - *Polypodium vulgare*
   Sea Spleenwort - *Asplenium marinum*

Wilson's Filmy-Fern - *Hymenophyllum wilsonii*
Flag, Yellow - *Iris pseudacorus*

Gentian, Field - *Gentianella campestris*
Grass, Creeping Bent - *Agrostis stolonifera*
   Early Hair-Grass - *Aira praecox*
   Common Bent - *Agrostis capillaris*
   Foxtail, Marsh - *Alopecurus geniculatus*
   Heath - *Danthonia decumbens*
   Mat - *Nardus stricta*
   Meadow, Annual - *Poa annua*
      Rough - *P. trivialis*
      Smooth - *P. pratensis*
   Oat-Grass, False - *Arrhenatherum elatius*
   Purple Moor - *Molinia caerulea*
   Red Fescue - *Festuca rubra*
   Rye - *Lolium perenne*
   Sheep's Fescue - *Festuca ovina*
   Sweet Vernal - *Anthoxanthum odoratum*
   Velvet Bent - *Agrostis canina*
   Viviparus Fescue - *Festuca vivipara*
   Wavy Hair - *Deschampsia flexuosa*
   Yorkshire Fog - *Holcus lanatus*

Hawksbit, Autumn - *Leontodon autumnalis*
Heather (Ling) - *Calluna vulgaris*
Heather, Bell - *Erica cinerea*
   Cross leaved heath - *Erica tetralix*
Honeysuckle, Common - *Lonicera periclymenum*
Horsetail, Common - *Equisetum arvense*

Lousewort - *Pedicularis sylvatica*

Milkwort, Common - *Polygala vulgaris*
Moss Campion - *Silene acaulis*
Moss, Sphagnum - *Sphagnum sp.*
   Woolly Hair - *Racomitrium sp.*
Mountain Everlasting - *Antennaria dioica*
Mouse-ear, Common - *Cerastium fontanum*
   Sea - *C. diffusum*

Nettle, Common - *Urtica dioica*

Orache, Babbington's - *Atriplex glabriuscula*
Orchid, Bog - *Hammarbya paludosa*
        Heath Spotted - *Dactylorhiza maculata*
        ericetorum

Pearlwort, Heath - *Sagina subulata*
        Procumbent - *S. procumbens*
Pennywort, Marsh - *Hydrocotyle vulgaris*
Pimpernel, Bog - *Anagallis tenella*
Plantain, Buck's-horn - *Plantago coronopus*
        Greater or Ratstail - *P. major*
        Ribwort - *P. lanceolata*
        Sea - *P. maritima*
Pondweed, Bog - *Potamogeton polygonifolius*
Primrose, Common - *Primula vulgaris*

Ragged Robin - *Lychnis flos-cuculi*
Ragwort, Common - *Senecio jacobaea*
Roseroot - *Sedum rosea*
Rush,   Black Bog - *Schoenus nigricans*
        Bulbous - *Juncus bulbosus*
        Common - *J. effusus*
        Heath - *J. squarrosus*
        Jointed - *J. articulatus*
        Toad - *J. bufonius*

Saxifrage, Purple - *Saxifraga oppositifolia*
Sea Campion - *Silene maritima*
Scabious, Devil's Bit - *Succisa pratensis*
Scentless Mayweed - *Matricaria maritima*
Scots Lovage - *Ligusticum scoticum*
Scurvy Grass - *Cochlearia officinalis*
Sedges, Carnation - *Carex panicea*
        Common - *C. nigra*
        Flea - *C. pulicaris*
        Glaucous - *C. flacca*
        Large, Yellow - *C. flava*
        Moor - *C. binervis*
        Pill - *C. pilulifera*

        Star - *C. echinata*
        Stiff - *C. bigelowii*
        Tawny - *C. hostiana*
        Yellow, Common - *C. demissa*
Self Heal - *Prunella vulgaris*
Silverweed - *Potentilla anserina*
Sneezewort - *Achillea ptarmica*
Sorrel, Common - *Rumex acetosa*
        Mountain - *Oxyria digyna*
        Sheep's - *Rumex acetosella*
Spearwort, Lesser - *Ranunculus flammula*
Speedwell, Common - *Veronica officinalis*
Spike-rush, Few flowered - *Eloecharis quinqueflora*
        Slender - *E. uniglumis*
Sow Thistle - *Sonchus asper*
St John's Wort, Elegant - *Hypericum pulchrum*
Starwort, Water - *Callitriche stagnalis*
Sundew, Common - *Drosera rotundifolia*
        Great - *D. anglica*

Thistle, Creeping - *Cirsium arvense*
        Spear - *C. vulgare*
Thrift (Sea Pink) - *Armeria maritima*
Thyme, Wild - *Thymus drucei*
Tormentil - *Potentilla erecta*

Vetch, Bush - *Vicia sepium*
Violet, Common Dog - *Viola riviniana*
        Marsh - *V. palustris*

Willow, Creeping - *Salix repens*
        Dwarf (or Least) - *S. herbacea*
Willow Herb, Marsh - *Epilobium palustre*
Woodrush, Great - *Luzula sylvatica*
        Field - *L. campestris*
        Heath - *L. multiflora*

Yarrow - *Achillea millefolium*
Yellow Rattle - *Rhinanthus minor*

Bird Checklist

BIRDS NESTING REGULARLY
SEABIRDS

Eider Duck - *Somateria mollissima*
Fulmar - *Fulmarus glacialis*
Gannet - *Sula bassana*
Guillemot,   Common - *Uria aalge*
             Black - *Cepphus grylle*
Gulls,   Great black-backed -
             Larus marinus
             Lesser black-backed -
             Larus fuscus
             Herring - *Larus argentatus*
Kittiwake - *Rissa tridactyla*
Puffin - *Fratercula arctica*
Petrel,   Leach's - *Oceanodroma
             leucorhoa*
             Storm - *Hydrobates
             pelagicus*
Razorbill - *Alca torda*
Shag - *Phalacrocorax artistotelis*
Shearwater, Manx - *Puffinus puffinus*
Skua, Great - *Stercorarius skua*

LAND AND WATER BIRDS

Crow, Hooded - *Corvus corone cornix*
Oystercatcher - *Haematopus ostralegus*
Pipit,   Meadow - *Anthus pratensis*
             Rock - *Anthus spinoletta*
Raven - *Corvus corax*
Snipe - *Gallinago gallinago*
Starling - *Sturnus vulgaris*
Wheatear - *Oenanthe oenanthe*
Wren, St Kilda - *Troglodytes troglodytes
hirtensis*

SEABIRD NUMBERS ON HIRTA (1987)

Fulmar (occupied sites)	35,000
Manx Shearwater	present
Storm Petrel	present
Leach's Petrel	present
Gannet	none
Shag	25 nests
Great Skua (territories)	44
Lesser B-b Gull (territories)	129
Herring Gull (territories)	14
Greater B-b (territories)	13
Kittiwake	2,000 sites
Guillemot (individuals)	10,000
Razorbill (individuals)	1,000
Black Guillemot	none
Puffin (occupied burrows)	11,000

TOTAL NUMBER OF SEABIRDS ON THE ISLANDS AND STACS OF ST KILDA (1987)

Fulmar (occupied sites)	63,000
Manx Shearwater	present
Storm Petrel	present
Leach's Petrel	present
Gannet (nests)	50,000
Shag (nests)	52
Great Skua (territories)	54
Lesser B-b Gull (territories)	154
Herring Gull (territories)	59
Greater B-b (territories)	56
Kittiwake	8,000 sites
Guillemot (individuals)	23,000
Razorbill (individuals)	4,000
Black Guillemot (individuals)	17
Puffin (occupied burrows)	230,000

Key to the Rocks of St Kilda

General appearance	Detailed colour	Features seen with a hand lens	Location	Identification
		Cream matrix, clear quartz, potassium feldspar crystals.	Conachair	
	Cream	A few black hornblende crystals. Some rocks with crystals in drusy cavities	Oiseval / Village Bay Shore	Conachair Granophyre
LIGHT ROCKS (acidic)	Light grey + dark flecks	White matrix of quartz, orthoclase, plagioclase, black hornblende	Mullach Sgar Complex between Glen + Village Bays	Micro-granite
	Grey + dark angular blocks	Grey matrix + flat clear crystals of plagioclase. Large, roughly rectangular grains of hornblende	Quarry	Hornblende Granophyre
GREY ROCKS (inter-mediate)	Grey-green	Fine texture, light feldspar + dark grey chlorite crystals evenly mixed, with a few small green-black hornblende crystals	Quarry / Dùn Passage / Na h-Eagan	Micro-diorite
	Uniformly dark	Fine grain, mainly dark pyroxenes + few light grey flecks of feldspar. Occasional pink orthoclase	Dùn Passage / Na h-Eagan (Cone sheets) / Village Bay	Dolerite
DARK ROCKS (basic)	Dark + pale grey streaks	Dolerite as above + grey + white crystals of acid intrusion fill, cracks from cooling	Dùn Passage / Na h-Eagan	Dolerite + Micro-granite
			Glen Bay Cambir (NW) Amhuinn Mór	Gabbro
	Mainly black + grey or green flecks	Coarse grain. Large black flat crystals of pyroxene. Olivine, honey coloured on weathered surface. Plagioclase generally white or pale grey	Glacan Mór Mullach Mór	Eucrite
			Mullach Bì Ruaival Dùn	Ultrabasic

THE ROCKS ON ST KILDA

The above descriptions are from collected specimens. The key uses fresh, not weathered rocks. There are variations from the above correlation of colour and rock name because identification on colour alone is not completely reliable. A more detailed study will require more specialised equipment.

Bibliography

BOOKS

Atkinson, R. *Island Going*, Collins, Glasgow, 1949

Baxter, C. and Crumley, J. *St Kilda. A portait of Britain's remotest island landscape*, Colin Baxter Photography, Lanark, 1988

Boyd, J. M. and Boyd, I. L. *The Hebrides*, Collins, Glasgow, 1990

Buchanan, Rev. J. L. *Travels in the Western Hebrides* from 1782-90, London, 1793

Buchanan, M. *St Kilda. A Photographic Album*, William Blackwood, Edinburgh, 1983

Charnley, B. *Last Greetings from St Kilda*, (Hebridean Heritage Series), Stenlake and McCourt, Glasgow, 1989

    A Voyage to St Kilda, Maclean Press, Skye, 1992

Coates, R. *The Place-names of St Kilda*, Edwin Mellen Press, Lampeter, 1990

Connell, R. *St Kilda and the St Kildans*, Hamilton, Adams & Co., London, 1887

Fisher, J. *The Fulmar*, New Naturalist Series, Collins, Glasgow, 1952

Harding, R. R., Merriman, R.J.and Nancarrow P. H. A. *St Kilda: An Illustrated Account of the Geology*, HMSO, London, 1984

Harris, M. P. *Birds of St Kilda*, Instit. of Terrestrial. Ecology., Cambridge, 1978

Harris, M. P. and Murray, S. *Birds of St Kilda*, HMSO, London,1989

Heathcote, N. *St Kilda*, Longman's Green and Co., 1900

Heathcote, N. *St Kilda*, Rowll Press, 1985

Jewell, P. A., Milner, C., Morton and Boyd, J. *Island Survivors*, University of London, 1974

Kearton, R. and C. *With Nature and a Camera*, Cassell and Co, 1897

Kennedy, J. *The Apostle of the North*, 1866, 2nd Ed., Free Presbyterian Pub., Glasgow, 1978

Macaulay, Rev. K. *History of St Kilda,1764*. Repr. Mercat Press, Edinburgh 1974

MacGregor, A. A. *A Last Voyage to St Kilda*, Cassell & Co., 1931

MacGregor, A. A. *The Furthest Hebrides*, Michael Joseph, London, 1969

Mackenzie, Rev. J. B. *Antiquities and Old Customs in St Kilda*, compiled from notes made by Rev. Neil MacKenzie, Minister on St Kilda 1829-43, Proc. Soc. Antiq. Scot 38, 1904

MacLean, C. *Island on the Edge of the World*, Canongate Press, Edinburgh, 1983

MacLean, L. *Sketches of the Island of St Kilda*, Glasgow, 1838

Martin, M. A. *Voyage to St Kilda*, 1697, 4th edition, Mercat Press, Edinburgh, 1986

    1698 A Late Voyage to St Kilda, Repr. Mackay 1934

Mitchell, W. R. *St Kilda – A Voyage to the Edge of the World*, Oban Times, Oban, 1990

Pike, O. G. *Through Birdland Byways with Pen and Camera*, Jarrold and Sons, 1910

Pike, O. G. *Nature and My Cine Camera*, Focal Press Ltd, 1946

Quine, D. A. *St Kilda Revisited*, Dowland Press, Frome, 1989

Quine, D. A. *St Kilda Portraits*, Dowland Press, Frome, 1988

Ridley, G. A. *Diver's Guide to St Kilda*, Gordon Ridley Publications, 1983

    St Kilda - A Submarine Guide, Privately Printed, 1983

    St Kilda - Diving Guides to Scotland, Nekton Books, 1994

Sands, J. *Out of this World or Life on St Kilda*, MacLachlan and Stewart, 1878

Seton, G. *St Kilda Past and Present*, Blackwood & Sons, 1878

Small, A. (editor) *A St Kilda Handbook*, The National Trust for Scotland, Edinburgh, 1979

Spackman, R. A. *Soldiers on St Kilda*, R.A. Range, Hebrides, 1982

Steel, T. *Life and Death of St Kilda*, Fontana, London, 1975, Revised 1988

Stell, G. P. and Harman, M., *Buildings of St Kilda*, Royal Commission of Ancient and
    Historical Monuments of Scotland, Edinburgh, 1988

Tasker, M. L., Moore, P. R. and Schofield, R. A. *Scottish Birds 15*, 1988
    The Seabirds of St Kilda, 1987

Thompson, F. *St Kilda and Other Hebridean Outliers*, David and Charles, Newton Abbot, 1988

Williamson, K. and Boyd, M. J. *St Kilda Summer*, Hutchinson, 1960

Williamson, K. and Boyd, M. J. *Mosaic of Islands*, Oliver and Boyd, 1963

Wilson, J. *A Voyage Round the Coasts of Scotland*, Adam and Charles Black, Edinburgh, 1842

OTHER REFERENCES

Barrington, R. M. *The Ascent of Stack-na-Biorrach, The Pointed Stack, St Kilda*, Alpine Journal,
    1913

Barry, J. *The Sunderland at the Head of Gleann Mór*, St Kilda Mail, 1980, *The Beaufighter
    Wreck on Conachair*, St Kilda Mail, 1981, *The Wellington on Soay*, St Kilda Mail, 1982,
    The Wellington Wreck on Soay, St Kilda Mail, 1988

Berry, R. J. *History in the Evolution of* Apodemus sylvaticas (Mammalia) *at One Edge of its
    Range*, Journal of Zoology 159, London, 1969

Berry, R. J. and Tricker, B. J. K., *Competition and Extinction: Mice of Foula, with Notes on
    Those on Fair Isle and St Kilda*, Journal of Zoology 158, London, 1969

Elwell, A. (Unpublished), *An Account of the Landing and Ascent of Soay*, St Kilda, 1993

Harman, M. *A Visit to Stac an Armin*, St Kilda Mail, 1982

Heathcote, N. *Scottish Climbing in St Kilda*, Scottish Mountaineering Club Journal, 1901

Kennedy, A. *Letter from St Kilda*, P.S.A.S., Vol 10, 1874

Lawson, B. *St Kilda and its Church*, Bill Lawson, Publications
    Croft History, Isle of St Kilda, Bill Lawson, Publications, 1993

Mackenzie, Rev. J. B. *Episode in the Life of the Rev. Neil MacKenzie at St Kilda from 1829-43*.
    Privately Printed, 1911

Meston, G. E. *My First Visit to St Kilda, 1934*, St Kilda Mail, 1992

Moore, P. *Gannet-hunters Bothy on Stac Lee, St Kilda*, Scottish Vernacular Buildings 11

Murray, G. *St Kilda Diary*, Unpublished, 1886-7

Murray, S. *A Count of Gannets on Boreray*, St Kilda Jour. Scot. Orni. Club ,Vol 11 No7,
    Autumn, 1981

Sands, J. 1877 (3 articles) *Life in St Kilda*, Chamber's Journal of Pop Lit, Sci and Art, May
    5,19,26, 1877

Sands, J., *Notes on the Antiquities of St Kilda*, P.S.A.S., Vol 12, 1877

Tasker, M. L., Moore, P. R. and Schofield, R. A., *The Seabirds of St Kilda, 1987*, Scot Birds,
    Vol 15,1988

Warren, J. *Stac Lee - An Account of its Ascent, May 1990*, Unpublished

Wigglesworth, J. *St Kilda and its Birds*, Liverpool, 1903

Index